Essential System Administration
Pocket Reference

Æleen Frisch

Beijing · Cambridge · Farnham · Köln · Paris · Sebastopol · Taipei · Tokyo

Essential System Administration Pocket Reference
by Æleen Frisch

Copyright © 2003 O'Reilly Media, Inc. All rights reserved.
Printed in the United States of America.

Published by O'Reilly Media, Inc., 1005 Gravenstein Highway North,
Sebastopol, CA 95472.

O'Reilly Media, Inc. books may be purchased for educational,
business, or sales promotional use. Online editions are also available
for most titles (*safari.oreilly.com*). For more information, contact our
corporate/institutional sales department: (800) 998-9938 or
corporate@oreilly.com.

Editor:	Mike Loukides
Production Editor:	Jane Ellin
Cover Designer:	Emma Colby
Interior Designer:	David Futato

Printing History:

    November 2002:   First Edition.

0-596-00449-4
[C]

Contents

Essential System Administration Pocket Reference

Introduction and Font Conventions

This book serves as a quick reference to the most important system administration commands, options, configuration files, and tasks on Unix systems, including specifics for AIX, FreeBSD, HP-UX, Linux, and Solaris. For more details about any item or topic, consult a general system administration reference (e.g., *Essential System Administration*, Third Edition, O'Reilly & Associates).

Items in this book are grouped by topic (see the Table of Contents). Within each topic, items are in more-or-less alphabetical order, although related items are kept together (use the Index to find any particular item).

This book uses the following font and symbol conventions:

Italic
> Used for the names of users and groups, files and directories, and replaceable parameters within normal text.

constant width bold
> Used for Unix commands, options, program names, and configuration-file literals and keywords.

constant width italic
> Used for replaceable parameters in commands, options, and configuration-file formats.

a|b
> Indicates a choice among items (e.g., a or b).

[optional]

> Optional items are enclosed in square brackets.

command†

> Open source commands are marked by a dagger.

The root Account

su   su [-] [*user*] [-c "*command*"]

> Run a command as another user (defaults to *root*). If no command is specified, a new shell is started. If the initial hyphen is included, then the user's login environment is duplicated.

Limiting access to su

AIX:	Limited to groups listed in the sugroups attribute for *root* in */etc/security/user*.
FreeBSD:	Define the member list for group 0 as non-null.
Linux:	Use the pam_wheel module in the su file.

su log file

AIX:	*/var/adm/sulog*	FreeBSD:	*/var/log/messages*
HP-UX:	*/var/adm/sulog*	Linux:	*/var/log/messages*
Solaris:	Specified in the SULOG setting in */etc/default/su*.		

Limiting direct root logins to the console

AIX:	chuser ttys="/dev/lft,/dev/tty0" rlogin=false root
FreeBSD:	Omit secure from all entries in */etc/ttys* except console.
HP-UX:	*/etc/securetty* lists devices where *root* is allowed to log in (omit "*/dev/*" from the names).
Linux:	Use the pam_securetty module.
Solaris:	*/etc/default/login*: CONSOLE=/dev/console

Granting Limited root Powers

sudo[†]   sudo [*options*] *command*

Run the specified command using the sudo facility. After successfully entering his password, a user can use the sudo command without having to re-enter it for a grace period (defaults to 5 minutes).

Options

-v   Reset the grace period to its full length.

-K   Terminate the grace period.

-u *user*   Run the command as the specified user (rather than *root*).

-l   List allowed commands for the current user and host.

Configuration file: /etc/sudoers

```
# alias definitions
Host_Alias NAME=host[,host…]        Named list of hosts
User_Alias NAME=user[,user…]        Named list of users
Cmnd_Alias NAME=cmd[,cmd…]          Named list of commands

# user access entries
user host = cmds [: host = cmds…]
```

The final line grants access to the specified commands on the indicated host. *User* is the name of a user, a group (precede its name with %), or previously-defined user alias, and *host* and *cmds* are lists of individual hosts/commands and/or defined aliases. Precede an item with ! to deny access.

The sudo package provides the visudo command for editing and validating the configuration file. Its log file is */var/adm/sudo.log*.

AIX system roles

System roles provide a way of assigning a subset of *root* privileges to a user.

Configuration file: /etc/security/roles

```
name:
[authorizations=list]
[rolelist=list]
[groups=name]
[screens=list]                    Allowed SMIT screens
```

A role is defined via the authorizations and/or rolelist attributes. groups sets the role's required group membership.

Assign a role with chuser roles=*role-list user*.

Authorizations

Backup
    Perform system backups.

Diagnostics
    Run system diagnostics.

GroupAdmin
    Manage administrative groups.

ListAuditClasses
    Display audit classes.

PasswdAdmin
    Change passwords for administrative users.

PasswdManage
    Change passwords for nonadministrative users.

Restore
    Restore system backups.

RoleAdmin
    Manage role definitions.

UserAdmin
    Add/remove all users; modify any account attributes.

UserAudit
    Modify any user account's auditing settings.

Defined roles

Required group follows role name in parentheses; component authorizations given after the description.

ManageBasicUsers (security)
Modify user audit settings (UserAudit, ListAuditClasses).

ManageAllUsers (security)
Add/remove user accounts; modify account attributes (User-Audit, ListAuditClasses, UserAdmin, RoleAdmin, Passwd-Admin, GroupAdmin).

ManageBasicPasswds (security)
Change ordinary users' passwords (PasswdManage).

ManageAllPasswds (security)
Change any password (PasswdManage, PasswdAdmin).

ManageRoles
Administer role definitions (RoleAdmin).

ManageBackup
Backup any files (Backup).

ManageBackupRestore
Backup or restore any files (Backup, Restore).

RunDiagnostics
Run diagnostic utilities; shutdown or reboot the system (Diagnostics).

ManageShutdown (shutdown)
Shutdown or reboot the system (no authorizations).

Solaris profiles and roles

Profiles and roles provide a way of assigning subsets of *root* privileges to users.

Profiles configuration file: /etc/security/prof_attr

Name:::*Desciption*:auths=*list*[,*attrib=value…*]

Defines profiles as groups of authorizations (defined in */etc/security/auth_attr*; */etc/security/exec_attr* maps profile components to commands and runtime UID/GIDs).

Important defined profiles

Basic Solaris User
Default authorizations.

Operator
Perform simple, low-risk administrative tasks.

System Administrator
Perform non–security-related administrative tasks.

Primary Administrator
Perform all administrative tasks.

Audit Control
Configure auditing.

Audit Review
Review auditing logs.

Cron Management
Manage at and cron jobs.

Device Management
Manage removable media.

Device Security
Manage devices and the Logical Volume Manager (LVM).

DHCP Management
Manage the DHCP service.

Filesystem Management
Mount and share filesystems.

Filesystem Security
Manage filesystem security attributes.

FTP Management
Manage the FTP server.

Mail Management
Manage sendmail and mail queues.

Media Backup
Backup files and filesystems.

Media Restore
Restore files from backups.

Name Service Management
Run non–security-related name-service commands.

Name Service Security
  Run security-related name-service commands.

Network Management
  Manage the host and network configuration.

Network Security
  Manage network and host security.

Object Access Management
  Change file ownership/permissions.

Printer Management
  Manage printers, daemons, and spooling.

Process Management
  Manage processes.

Software Installation
  Add application software to the system.

User Management
  Manage users and groups (except passwords).

User Security
  Manage all aspects of users and groups.

Assigning profiles to user accounts

Performed in the */etc/user_attr* configuration file:

```
user::::type=normal|role,attribute=value ...
```

type indicates whether the entry assigns items to a user or defines
a role. Attributes include:

```
profiles=list
```
  Assign the specified profiles to the user.

```
roles=list
```
  Assign the specified roles to the user.

```
auths=list
```
  Grant the specified individual authorizations to the user.

```
project=list
```
  Assign the user to a project (used for accounting purposes).

Default authorizations and profiles

Default authorizations and profiles are assigned in */etc/security/policy.conf*:

```
AUTHS_GRANTED=list
PROFS_GRANTED=list
```

Displaying profiles, roles, and authorizations

Use the profiles, roles, and auths commands (respectively).

Essential Administrative Tools

Vendor-provided system administration tools

The various operating systems provide the following GUI and menu-driven administrative tools.

AIX:	smit, wsm	HP-UX:	sam
FreeBSD:	sysinstall	Solaris:	admintool, smc
Linux:	redhat-config-* (Red Hat); yast2 (SuSE)		

---

chroot   chroot *directory command*

Change the root to the specified directory, and then execute the specified command. The command will interpret all paths as starting from the specified directory (rather than /).

---

date   date *MMDDhhmm*[*CC*]*YY*[.*ss*]

Set the date and time (using a 24-hour clock). For example, the argument for 1:47 p.m. on September 5, 2002 is 0905134702.

---

file   file *files*

List the types of each specified file. Identification is made based on the "magic numbers" defined in the *magic* configuration file (its location varies by system).

---

find   find *starting-dirs* [*matching-criteria-and-actions*]

Locate files that have the specified characteristics, and perform the specified actions on each file. *Starting-dirs* is a list of one or more directories from which to start searching. If the matching-criteria expression returns a true value; then the specified actions are carried out on the matching file.

Matching-criteria options

-atime *n*
> The file was last accessed exactly *n* days ago.

-mtime *n*
> The file was last modified exactly *n* days ago.

-newer *file*
> The file was modified more recently than *file*.

-size *n*
> The file is *n* 512-byte blocks long (rounded up to next block).

-links *n*
> The file's inode has exactly *n* hard links.

-type *c*
> Specifies the file type: f (plain file), d (directory), l (symbolic link), p (named pipe), s (socket), b (block special file), c (character special file).

-fstype *type*
> Specifies the filesystem type.

-name *fname*
> The filename is *fname*.

-perm [-]*p*
> The file's numeric access mode is *p*. If the hyphen is included, then only the bits set in *p* are compared to the file's access mode, and all other permissions are ignored.

-user *username*
> The file's owner is *username*.

-group *grpname*

>   The file's group owner is *grpname*.

-nouser

>   The file's owner is not listed in the password file.

-nogroup

>   The file's group owner is not listed in the group file.

Numeric options can be preceded by + or -, which signify "more than" and "less than," respectively (e.g., -mtime +3 means "modified more than 3 days ago").

Action options

-print

>   Display the pathname of the matching file. This is the default when no action option is included.

-ls

>   Display the long directory listing for the matching file.

-exec *cmd*
-ok *cmd*

>   Execute the specified command on the file. Use the {} construct to place the filename into the command. The command must end with an escaped semicolon (\;). The -ok form issues a prompt before executing the command on each file.

-xdev

>   Restrict the search to the filesystem of the starting directory (typically used to bypass mounted remote filesystems).

-prune

>   Don't descend into any directories that are encountered.

Forming complex expressions

-a   Join matching-criteria options with AND logic. This is the default (i.e., all relevant options must return true for a file to match if no explicit connecting options are specified).

-o   Join options/expressions with OR logic.

\!   Negate the result of an option/expression.

\(\)
     Parentheses are used for explicit grouping.

---

grep   grep [options] pattern [files]

Search the listed files (or standard input) for lines that match the pattern and print those lines.

Options

-c   Print only the number (count) of matching lines.

-h   Don't label matching lines with the filename (applies only when searching multiple files).

-i   Perform a case-insensitive comparison.

-l   Print only the names of files that contain matching lines.

-n   Precede each matching line with its line number in the file.

-v   Print nonmatching lines instead of matching ones.

Regular expression overview

Most characters are interpreted literally. The following constructs may also be used:

.   Match any single character.

^   Match the beginning of the line.

$ Match the end of the line.

\x   Match regular expression special characters (e.g., \$ matches a literal dollar sign).

[list]
     Match any character in the list. The list may include ranges (e.g., 0-9). If the first character is a caret (^), any character that is not in the list matches. Place a literal] first in the list, a literal - last in the list, and a literal ^ anywhere but first.

( )
> Group subpatterns.

?
> Match exactly one of the preceding item.

*
> Match zero or more of the preceding item.

+
> Match one or more of the preceding item.

{n} Match exactly *n* of the preceding item.

{n,}
> Match *n* or more of the preceding item.

{n,m}
> Match at least *n*, but no more than *m*, of the preceding item.

|
> Match one or both of the preceding and following items.

makewhatis

```
makewhatis [-a] [man-directory]    Most Unix systems
catman -w [-M man-directory]        Solaris
```

Generate the manual-pages index file, using the default or specified manual-pages directory tree. Use the makewhatis -a option to append new entries to the existing index rather than recreating the index from scratch.

startsrc, stopsrc, and lssrc (AIX)

```
command [options]
```

Start/stop/display information about a daemon or group of daemons managed by the System Resource Controller (SRC).

Options

-s server
> Limit action to the specified server.

-g server-group
> Perform the action for all servers in the specified server group.

-a *args* (startsrc)

Pass arguments to the daemon process on startup.

-a *(*lssrc *and* stopsrc*)*

Display information for/stop all servers.

-h *host*

Perform the operation on the specified host.

-p *PID*

With lssrc and stopsrc, this option says to operate on this specific instance of a server. However, if *PID* refers to an SRC server process, then the request is sent to the specific SRC instance for all three commands.

Starting the SRC itself

scrmstr

Start an instance of the SRC.

---

xargs   xargs [*options*] *command*

Repeat execution of the specified command, appending each item from standard input to *command.*

Options

-i[*cc*]

Place the incoming items within the command. The characters *cc* specify the placeholder characters; they default to {}.

-n*n* Send incoming arguments to the command in groups of *n*.

-p   Issue a prompt before executing each command.

-t   Display each command prior to executing it.

-c '*command*'

Specify a command that contains space and/or special characters.

Package management commands

List all installed packages

AIX:	`lslpp -l all`	FreeBSD:	`pkg_info -a -I`
HP-UX:	`swlist`	Linux:	`rpm -q -a`
Solaris:	`pkginfo`		

Describe a package

FreeBSD:	`pkg_info pkg`	HP-UX:	`swlist -v pkg`
Linux:	`rpm -q -i pkg`	Solaris:	`pkginfo -l pkg`

List package contents

AIX:	`lslpp -f pkg`	FreeBSD:	`pkg_info -L pkg`
HP-UX:	`swlist -l pkg`	Linux:	`rpm -q -l pkg`
Solaris:	`pkgchk -l pkg`		

List package prerequisites

AIX:	`lslpp -p pkg`	Linux:	`rpm -q --requires pkg`

Show package a file belongs to

AIX:	`lslpp -w file`	Solaris:	`pkgchk -l -p file`
Linux:	`rpm -q --whatprovides file`		

List available packages on media

AIX:	`installp -ld dev`	FreeBSD:	`sysinstall`
HP-UX:	`swlist -s path`	Linux:	`ls path-to-rpms`
Solaris:	`ls /path-to-pkgs`	Linux:	`yast2` (SuSE)

Install a package

AIX:	`installp -acX pkg`	FreeBSD:	`pkg_add pkg`
HP-UX:	`swinstall pkg`	Linux:	`rpm -i pkg`
Solaris:	`pkgadd pkg`		

Preview package installation

AIX:	`installp -p pkg`	FreeBSD:	`pkg_add -n pkg`
HP-UX:	`swinstall -p pkg`	Linux:	`rpm -i --test pkg`

Verify an installed package

AIX:	`installp -a -v pkg`	Linux:	`rpm -V pkg`
Solaris:	`pkgchk pkg`		

Remove a package

AIX:	installp -u *pkg*	FreeBSD:	pkg_delete *pkg*
HP-UX:	swremove *pkg*	Linux:	rpm -e *pkg*
Solaris:	pkgrm *pkg*		

Devices and Device Files

dmesg   dmesg   *Not available under AIX*

Display boot and other system messages. Devices are listed within the messages as the devices are detected.

Vendor-specific device listing commands

AIX:	lscfg	*List all devices.*
	lsdev -C -s scsi	*List all SCSI devices.*
	lscfg -v -l *device*	*Display device details.*
	lsattr -E -H -l *device*	*Display device attributes.*
FreeBSD:	pciconf -l -v	*List PCI devices.*
	camcontrol devlist	*List SCSI devices.*
	usbdevs	*List USB devices.*
HP-UX:	ioscan -f -n	*Display detailed device listing.*
	ioscan -f -n -C disk	*Limit to device class.*
Linux:	lsdev	*List major devices.*
	scsiinfo -l	*List SCSI devices.*
	lspci	*List PCI devices.*
	lsusb	*List USB devices.*
Solaris:	getdev	*List devices.*
	getdev type=*class*	*Limit to device class.*
	devattr -v *device*	*Display device detail.*

Special File Formats

In all cases, the optional *r* in special filenames refers to the character device (i.e., raw access mode), and the other name refers to the block device.

Disk partition special filenames

AIX: /dev/hdiskn (refers to entire disk)

n is the disk number. Example: */dev/hdisk1*

FreeBSD: /dev/[r]ppnsmx (often shortened to /dev/[r]ppnx)

pp is a device-specific prefix (e.g., *ad* or *wd* for IDE disks, *da* for SCSI), *n* is the disk number, *m* is the slice number (physical partition), and *x* is the partition letter. Example: */dev/da1s1a*

HP-UX: /dev/[r]dsk/cktidn

k is the controller number, *i* is the SCSI ID, and *n* is the disk number. Example: */dev/dsk/c0t4d1*

Linux: /dev/[sd|hd]ym

The *sd/hd* prefix refers to SCSI/IDE disks, respectively, *y* is the disk letter (where *a* refers to the first disk, etc.), and *m* is the physical partition number. Example: */dev/hda1*

Solaris: /dev/[r]dsk/cktid0sm

k is the controller number, *i* is the SCSI ID, and *m* is the physical partition number. Example: */dev/dsk/c0t4d0s2*

CD-ROM device special filenames

AIX:	*/dev/cd0*	HP-UX:	*/dev/dsk/cktid0*
Linux:	*/dev/cdrom*	Solaris:	*/dev/dsk/c0tid0s02*
FreeBSD:	*/dev/cd0c* (SCSI), */dev/acd0c* (ATAPI)		

For HP-UX and Solaris, *k* and *i* have the same meanings in special filenames for both disks and CD-ROMs.

Floppy disk special filenames

AIX:	*/dev/fd0*	FreeBSD:	*/dev/fd0*
HP-UX:	*/dev/dsk/c0t1d0*	Linux:	*/dev/fd0*
Solaris:	*/dev/diskette*		

Network interface names

The following list indicates the first network interface. Additional interfaces will have higher numbers (e.g., *eth1*).

AIX:	*en0*	FreeBSD:	*xl0*, *de0* (and others)
HP-UX:	*lan0*	Linux:	*eth0*
Solaris:	*hme0*, *dnet0*, *eri0*, *le0* (and others)		

Tape special filenames

k is the drive number, and n means "no rewind" in all cases.

AIX: /dev/rmt*k*[.*m*]

    m is a suffix indicating rewind, retensioning, and density settings (see the rmt(4) man page). The default is rewind, no retension, and low density.

FreeBSD: /dev/[n]rast*k* and /dev/[e|n]rsa*k*

    e means "eject tape on close."

HP-UX: /dev/rmt/c*i*t*j*d0*TYPE*[b][n]

    i is the controller number, *j* is the SCSI ID, b says to use BSD-style error control, and *TYPE* is a keyword that indicates the tape type and/or density (e.g., BEST, DDS). */dev/rmt* often contains links between these names and simpler ones (e.g., *0m* linked to *c0t3d0BEST*).

Linux: /dev/[n]st*k*[*x*]

    x indicates the density selection: l, m, and a for low, medium, and autoselect, respectively.

Solaris: /dev/rmt/*k*[*x*][b][n][c]

    b says to use BSD-style error control, *x* indicates the density (l, m, and h for low, medium, and high, respectively), and c says to use hardware compression.

Default tape drive

AIX:	*/dev/rmt0*	FreeBSD:	*/dev/rsa0*
HP-UX:	*/dev/rmt/0m*	Linux:	*/dev/st0*
Solaris:	*/dev/rmt/0*		

Modifying tape drive settings under AIX

```
lsattr -E -H -l device
```
    Display attributes to the specified tape drive.

```
chdev -l rmtn -a block_size=bytes -a compress=yes|no \
-a ret=yes|no
```
    Change settings of the specified tape drive.

Serial line special files

The following table gives the form for the first device of each type:

	Serial line	Dial-out form	Slave pseudo terminal
AIX:	/dev/tty0	/dev/tty0	/dev/pts/0
FreeBSD:	/dev/ttyd0	/dev/cuaa0	/dev/ttyp0
HP-UX:	/dev/tty0p0	/dev/cua0p0	/dev/ttyd0p0, /dev/pts/0
Linux:	/dev/ttyS0	/dev/ttyS0	/dev/ttyp0
Solaris:	/dev/term/a	/dev/cua/0	/dev/pts/0

System console: /dev/console
> System console device. On AIX systems, the console device in terminal mode is */dev/lft0*.

Printer special filenames

First parallel port devices:

AIX:	/dev/lp0	FreeBSD:	/dev/lpt0
HP-UX:	/dev/lp	Solaris:	/dev/ecpp0
Linux:	/dev/parport0 (usually mapped to /dev/lp0)		

USB device special files

The following list shows the first file of each type.

Mouse

FreeBSD:	/dev/ums0	Solaris:	/dev/usbms
Linux:	/dev/input/mouse0 and /dev/input/mice		

Zip drive

FreeBSD:	/dev/da0s4	Linux:	/dev/sda4
Solaris:	/dev/dsk/c1t0d0s0:c		

Printer

FreeBSD:	/dev/ulpt0	Linux:	/dev/usblp0
Solaris:	/dev/usbprn0		

Other devices found on some systems

/dev/null
    Null device (discards all output; reads return 0 bytes).

/dev/zero
    Returns a zero-filler buffer.

/dev/random
    Random number generator.

File Ownership and Protection

chmod   chmod [-R] *access-string*[,*access-string...*] *files*

Change the file mode of the specified files as directed in the *access-string*. -R operates recursively on any directories in the file list.

Access-string can be a numeric file mode or one or more symbolic permission strings; symbolic permission strings have the general syntax:

    [*class*]+|-|=[*type*]

where *class* is one or more access class code letters: u for user, g for group, o for other, a for all. a is the default (although on some systems, omitting the access class causes the specified permissions to be limited by the current umask).

The second item is an operator: + to add permissions, - to remove them, and = to set permissions to the specified value.

Type is one or more access type code letters: r (read), x (execute), w (write), or one of the special types listed in the following section.

Special access types

X   Set execute access only if it has already been set for some access class.

t *(save text mode/sticky bit) [numeric 1000]*
> When used for other access on a directory, restricts user file deletions to his own files.

s *(SetUID and SetGID) [numeric 4000 and 2000]*
> When used with user and group access, causes a program to execute in the user/group context of the files's owner(s), rather than the user who ran it. Both require the corresponding execute access to be on.
>
> SetGID access on a directory causes new file group ownership to follow the directory's group owner rather than the primary group of the creating user.

l *(file locking: Solaris, some Linux) [numeric 2000]*
> Set mandatory file locking on reads/writes. Assign via the group access class; requires that group execute access is off.

---

chown   chown [-R] *new-owner*[:*new-group*] *files*
chgrp   chgrp [-R] *new-group files*

Change the user/group ownership of the specified files. The -R option performs a recursive operation on directories in *files*.

---

umask   umask *mask*

Set the default permission mode mask (the corresponding default mode is the octal compliment of *mask*).

Access Control Lists (ACLs)

AIX ACLs

acledit
> Edit ACL interactively. The ACL has this basic format:

attributes:	*Special mode keywords (e.g., SetUID)*
base permissions	*Normal Unix file modes:*
owner(user): ppp	*User access*
group(group): ppp	*Group access*
others: ppp	*Other access*

```
        extended permissions  More specific permission entries:
          enabled|disabled         Whether they're used or not
          op ppp u|g:name[,…]     Access control entry (ACE)
```

where *ppp* is the usual permission string (e.g., rwx).

Within ACEs, *op* is one of specify, deny, or permit (indicating how the entry should be applied), and *name* is the user/group to which it applies (depending on whether u or g is the first character). Multiple items within the list must all match for it to apply.

aclget [-o *file*] *acl-source*
> View the ACL for the specified source file (-o writes it to *file*).

aclput [-i *file*] *acl-target(s)*
> Apply the ACL on standard input (or in *file*) to the target file(s).

ACL interpretation

All applicable entries are unioned; access is denied unless it is both explicitly permitted and not explicitly denied.

HP-UX ACLs

lsacl *file(s)*
> Display ACLs.

chacl *user.group* = *ppp* *file-list*
> Modify the ACL for the specified files (add -r to replace it instead). *ppp* is the usual permission string (e.g., rwx).
>
> % can be used as a wildcard for the user and/or group; an at symbol (@) serves as shorthand for the current user/group.

chmod -A …
> Change Unix permissions without erasing the existing ACL.

ACL interpretation

The first applicable entry determines the allowed access. Entries are examined in order of decreasing specificity: entries with a specific user and group, then ones with just a specific user, then entries with only a specific group, and, finally, the other permission. Within a class, entries are examined in order.

POSIX ACLs (Linux and Solaris)

Access control entry format

c:[*name*]:*ppp*

ppp is the usual access mode string. *c* is a code letter that indicates the entry type: u (user), g (group), o (other), or m (mask). *Name* is omitted for u and g to refer to the user and group owners (two colons follow them); *name* and the following colon are omitted with o.

The mask ACE sets the maximum access level allowed for all but user owner and other access.

On Solaris systems, the ACE syntax adds a d: prefix to the entry for directory default ACEs (which apply to new files).

Linux filesystems with ACLs must be mounted with -o acl.

Commands (add the target file list to each one)

Add/modify ACEs:
Linux: setfacl -m *ACEs*   Solaris: setfacl -m *ACEs*

Replace ACL:
Linux: setfacl -s *ACEs*   Solaris: setfacl -s *ACEs*

Take ACL data from a file:
Linux: setfacl -M|-S *acl-file*
Solaris: setfacl -m|-s -f *acl-file*

Remove ACEs:
Linux: setfacl -x *ACEs*   Solaris: setfacl -d *ACEs*

Remove entire ACL:
Linux: setfacl -b

Operate on directory default ACL:
Linux: setfacl -d *ACEs*   Solaris: setfacl [*options*] d:*ACE*

Remove default ACL:
Linux: setfacl -k

ACL interpretation

- The user owner uses only u:: (all group ACEs are ignored).
- Any user with a specific u: entry always uses that entry (group entries are ignored), subject to the mask ACE limits.

- Users without specific entries applying group entries:
  - Under Solaris, applicable group entries are combined.
  - On Linux systems, group entries do not accumulate. Users can use any one applicable group entry.

  The mask limits the access acquired from group ACEs.
- Everyone else uses the specified other access.

System Messages and Log Files

File locations

syslog daemon configuration file

Usual: */etc/syslog.conf*

General message log file

Usual: */var/log/messages*
HP-UX: */var/adm/syslog/syslog.log*
Solaris: */var/adm/messages*

syslog subsystem configuration

FreeBSD: */etc/rc.conf*: syslogd_enable and syslogd_flag.
Linux: */etc/sysconfig/syslog* (SuSE):
          SYSLOGD_PARAMS and KERNEL_LOGLEVEL.

/etc/syslog.conf file format

facility[,*facility*].*level*[;*facilities*.*level*]   *dest*

Facility is a list of one or more defined syslog "facilities," which are sources of system messages. Multiple facilities are separated by commas.

Level is a defined message severity level; all messages at that level and higher will be selected.

Multiple facility-level pairs may be listed, separated by semicolons. An asterisk may be used for either item; the asterisk refers to all facilities or all severity levels, except mark.

The final item is the message destination; it can be a full pathname to a file, a user or list of users to whom a message should be sent (* refers to all logged-in users), or @*hostname* (forward it to the syslog daemon on that host). Note that specified files must already exist.

Facilities

kern	The kernel.
user	User processes.
mail	The mail subsystem.
lpr	The printing subsystem.
daemon	System server processes.
auth	The user authentication system (nonsensitive information).
authpriv	The user authentication system (security sensitive information). Some systems have only one of auth and authpriv.
mark	Internal syslog time stamp messages (generated every 20 minutes by default).
local*	Eight local message facilities (0–7). Some operating systems define one or more of them.

Some systems define additional subsystem-specific facilities, such as ftp, news, uucp, syslog, etc.

Severity levels

emerg	System panic.
alert	Serious errors that require immediate attention.
crit	Critical errors, such as hard device errors.
err	Other errors.
warning	Warnings.
notice	Noncritical messages.
info	Informative messages.

debug	Extra information that is helpful for tracking down problems.
none	Ignore messages from this facility.
mark	Selects timestamp messages. The asterisk wildcard does not include this facility.

AIX enhancements to syslog

AIX adds additional fields to *syslog.conf* entries:

```
… rotate [size s] [files n] [time t] [compress]
[archive path]
```

The rotate keyword introduces the other log file rotation options.

size *s*
: Size threshold for automatic log file rotation. Rotate the log when it is larger than *s*. Follow *s* by k or m for KB or MB.

files *n*
: Retain the *n* most recent files.

time *t*
: Time threshold. Rotate the log when older than *t*. Follow *t* by h, d, w, m, or y for hours, days, weeks, months, or years, respectively.

compress
: Compress old files.

archive *path*
: Move rotated files to the specified directory location.

FreeBSD and Linux syntax enhancements

facility.=*severity*
: Severity level is exactly the one specified.

facility.!=*severity (Linux only)*
: Severity level is anything other than the one specified.

facility.<*severity (FreeBSD only)*
: Severity level is lower than the one specified. The .<= and .> comparison operators are also provided (as is .>=).

|command
> Additional destination type. Pipe the message to *command*.

Additional FreeBSD syslog.conf entry types

+host and -host
> Subsequent entries apply/don't apply to the specified host. Note that host entries accumulate; use +@ to reset the host list to the local system.

!command
> Subsequent entries apply only to messages from the specified command. Command entries accumulate; use !* to reset the list to all commands.

Solaris enhancements to syslog.conf syntax

Solaris integrates m4 macros into *syslog.conf*. For example:

```
mail.debug    ifdef(`LOGHOST', /var/log/syslog,
@loghost)
```

Consult the documentation for the m4 package for details.

---

syslogd syslogd [*options*]

> The syslog daemon. Available options vary by operating system. The most important option rejects incoming syslog messages from remote systems:

AIX:	-r	FreeBSD:	-s
HP-UX:	-N	Solaris:	-t
Linux:	-r *accepts* remote messages (rejected by default).		

---

logger logger [*options*] "*message*"

> Send a message to the syslog facility.

Options

-p *facility.severity*
> Specify facility and severity level.

-t *tag*
> Mark all message lines with the specified tag string.

-i
> Include the process ID in the syslog message.

logrotate[†]

```
logrotate [options] config-file
```

Rotate log files based on the instructions in the specified configuration file (*/etc/logrotate.conf* by default). Use the -f option to force rotation unconditionally. (Included with Linux systems.)

Configuration file general syntax

global settings and defaults

```
log-file-path {
  specific settings
}
```

Configuration file directives

errors *user*
> Mail errors to the specified user.

compress | nocompress
> Compress/don't compress the rotated saved logs.

create [*mode* [*owner* [*group*]]]
> After rotation, recreate the log file with the specified permissions and/or ownerships.

rotate *n*
> Keep *n* old log files.

size *s*[M|k]
> Rotate only logs that are larger than *s* bytes (no suffix), MB, or KB.

daily, weekly, monthly
> Rotate the log on the first run of the day, week, or month.

olddir *directory*
> Place the rotated log file in the specified directory.

```
prerotate|postrotate
  commands
endscript
```
> Run the specified commands before/after rotating the log.

include *directory*
> Import the configuration files in the specified directory.

See the logrotate documentation for other directives.

The AIX error log

The AIX binary error log file is maintained by the errdemon daemon in */var/adm/ras/errlog*. The relevant commands are:

errpt
> Report on errors in the error log.

errclear *n*
> Remove all errors more than *n* days old from the error log.

The HP-UX error log

The HP-UX error log is stored in a series of files: */var/stm/logs/os/log.*.raw** (binary format). View the data using the xstm (GUI), mstm (menu-driven), and cstm (command-line) utilities.

swatch[†] swatch [-c *config-file*] [*options*]

> Examine the item specified in the option for patterns, as defined in the configuration file (defaults *$HOME/.swatchrc*).

Options

-t *file*   Examine ("tail") the end of the specified file continuously.

-f *file*   Examine the specified file once.

-p *command* Examine the output of the specified command.

Configuration file format

```
watchfor /reg-exp/
    directives
```

Configuration file directives

echo | bell
> Display matching lines. bell also rings the bell.

throttle [hours:]minutes:seconds
> Ignore duplicate messages for the specified period of time.

exec command
> Execute the specified command when a match is found.

mail [addresses=user[:user…][,subject=text]]
> Send mail to the specified users when a match is found.

write user[:user…]
> Send a message to the specified user(s).

,when weekdays:hours
> Used as suffix to other action directives, limiting their scope to the specified day, range of days (Monday=1), and/or hour(s).

See the documentation for full details about the configuration file.

Startup and Shutdown

Booting the system manually

AIX
> Little intervention is allowed. Boot from an alternate device by using the AIX bootlist command to set the device order.

FreeBSD
> Select a disk and/or partition from the menu. Strike a key when prompted; then use the boot command (add -s for

single-user mode). To boot an alternate kernel, use commands like:

```
unload
load filename
boot
```

HP-UX (> prompt)

List devices with the search command. Use bo *xx* to boot the device labeled *xx* in the search output (e.g., CD-ROM).

HP-UX (ISL> prompt)

Use the hpux command. Add -is (for single-user mode) and/ or a pathname to boot an alternate kernel.

Linux (lilo boot loader)

The Tab key lists the boot choices; enter one choice to boot (e.g., linux). Add single to boot to single-user mode.

Linux (grub boot loader)

Use the following commands to specify all boot parameters:

```
grub> root (hd0,0)                    Partition to boot from
grub> kernel path ro root=/dev/xdyn   Kernel /root devs
grub> initrd path                     If needed
grub> boot                            Initiate the boot
```

When specifying the root device, *x* is either h or s, *y* is the disk letter, and *n* is the partition number.

Solaris

Enter L1-a or Stop-a to get the ok prompt. From there, the boot command starts a boot (-s selects single-user mode). The boot cdrom command boots from CD-ROM.

System V-style run levels

0	Halted state: conditions when it is safe to turn off the power.
1	System administration/maintenance state.
S and s	Single-user mode.
2	Multiuser mode (AIX default).
3	Remote file-sharing state (HP-UX and Solaris default).

4, 7, 8, 9	Administrator-definable system states. HP-UX and Solaris do not support run levels 7 through 9.
5	Same as run level 3 but running a graphical login program on the system console (Linux default).
6	Shutdown and reboot state.
Q and q	Pseudo-state that tells init to reread its configuration file.
a, b, c	Pseudo–run levels that can be defined locally. When invoked, they cause init to run the commands in /etc/inittab without changing the current (numeric) run level.

Default run level

Set in the initdefault entry in /etc/initttab.

Viewing the current run level

Usual: who -r   Linux: runlevel

---

init   init r

Take the system to run level r, as directed by the corresponding entries in the /etc/inittab configuration file.

Configuration file: /etc/inittab

The general entry syntax is:

    cc:levels:action:process

where cc is a label (conventionally, 2 characters, but all of our systems allow at least 4 characters), levels is a concatenated list of run-level characters to which the entry applies, action is a keyword that indicates how init is to manage the corresponding process (see the following section), and process is the command to run.

Action keywords

wait

Start the process and wait for it to finish before going on to the next entry for this run state.

---

respawn

> Start the process and restart it automatically when it dies (commonly used for getty terminal-line server processes).

once

> Start the process if it isn't already running. Don't wait for it.

boot

> Execute the entry only at boot time; start the process, but don't wait for it.

bootwait

> Execute the entry only at boot time and wait for it to finish.

initdefault

> Specify the default run level (the one to reboot to).

sysinit

> Used for activities that need to be performed before init tries to access the system console (for example, initializing the appropriate device).

off

> If the process associated with this entry is running, kill it. off is also used to comment out unused terminal lines.

Enabling single-user mode password protection

AIX and HP-UX

> Automatic.

FreeBSD

> Use the insecure option in the console entry in /etc/ttys:
>
>   console none unknown off insecure

Linux

> Include an entry for sulogin in /etc/inittab:
>
>   sp:S:respawn:/sbin/sulogin

Solaris

> Use PASSREQ="YES" in /etc/default/sulogin.

Boot script locations

Main boot script

AIX:	/etc/rc	FreeBSD:	/etc/rc
HP-UX:	/sbin/rc	Linux:	/etc/rc.d/rc
Solaris:	/sbin/rcn		

Secondary boot scripts/script directories

AIX:	/etc/rc.*	FreeBSD:	/etc/rc.*
HP-UX:	/sbin/rcn.d and /sbin/init.d		
Linux:	/etc/rc.d/rcn.d and /etc/init.d (Red Hat);		
	/etc/init.d/rcn.d and /etc/init.d (SuSE)		
Solaris:	/etc/rcn.d and /etc/init.d		

Boot script configuration files

FreeBSD:	/etc/rc.conf	HP-UX:	/etc/rc.config.d/*
Linux:	/etc/sysconfig/*	Solaris:	/etc/default/*

shutdown

System V-style shutdown command

```
shutdown [-y] [-g grace] [-i r] message   Solaris
shutdown [-y] grace                        HP-UX
```

Grace is the grace period before the shutdown process starts (default is 60 seconds under Solaris). -y says to answer all prompts with "yes" automatically. -i specifies the new run level (defaults to S). *Message* is a message sent to all logged-in users.

HP-UX /etc/shutdown.allow configuration file

This file specifies who can shut down the system. It contains entries of the form:

    host   user

which allows the specified user to shut down the indicated host. The plus sign (+) can be used as a wildcard.

BSD-style shutdown command

shutdown [*options*] *when message*   *BSD-style command.*

Shut down to single-user mode. *When* indicates when the shutdown should start. It has the three forms: +*m* (in *m* minutes), *h*:*m* (at this time, using a 24-hour clock), and now. *Message* is a message sent to all logged-in users.

Options

-r   Reboot to multiuser mode after shutting down.

-h   Halt the processor after shutting down.

-k   Fake shutdown; the message is sent, but the system stays up.

-m *(AIX)*
      Shut down to single-user mode (halted state is the default).

-t *secs (Linux)*
      Specify the delay between sending the TERM and KILL signals to processes (the default is 30 seconds).

-a *(Linux)*
      Requires that a user listed in */etc/shutdown.allow* be logged in on the console (or virtual console). Otherwise, the command is ignored.

-c *(Linux)*
      Cancel a pending shutdown.

---

sync   sync; sync [; sync …]

Flush unwritten buffers to disk.

User Accounts

/etc/passwd   The password file

username:x:*UID*:*GID*:*user-info*:*home-dir*:*login-shell*

username   User account login name (generally limited to 8 characters).

---

x	Traditional password field, set to a fixed character (usually x) when a shadow password file is in use. AIX uses an exclamation point (!), and FreeBSD uses an asterisk (*).
UID	The user identification number.
GID	The user's primary group membership.
user-info	Conventionally, contains the user's full name and, possibly, other job-related information (e.g., office location or phone number). Up to five comma-separated subfields may be defined.
home-dir	The user's home directory.
login-shell	The program used as the command interpreter for this user. On most systems, the */etc/shells* file lists the full pathnames of valid shell programs; on AIX systems, valid shells are listed in the shells field in the usw stanza of */etc/security/login.cfg*:

```
shells = /bin/sh, /bin/csh, …
```

Shadow password files

/etc/shadow (Linux and Solaris)

user:*pwd*:*changed*:*minlife*:*maxlife*:*warn*:*inactive*:*expires*:

user	Username (as in */etc/passwd*).
pwd	Encoded password.
changed	Last password change (Unix date format[*]).
minlife	Minimum number of days a user must keep a new password.
maxlife	Maximum password lifetime, in days.
warn	Days to warn in advance of an upcoming password expiration.

---

[*] Unix systems often store dates as the number of seconds (or milliseconds) since midnight on 1/1/1970.

| *inactive* | Days after password expiration that the account will be disabled. |
| *expires* | Date the account expires (Unix date format). |

/etc/master.passwd (FreeBSD)

```
user:pwd:UID:GID:class:pwd-expire:acct-expire:
user-info:…
```

This file, which serves as both *passwd* and *shadow* files, uses three additional fields between the GID and user information fields:

pwd	Encoded password.
class	User class (see page 37).
pwd-expire	Password expiration date (Unix date format).
acct-expire	Account expiration date (Unix date format).

/etc/security/passwd (AIX)

Encoded passwords are stored in the password field.

/etc/group   The group file

```
name:*:GID:additional-members
```

name	Group name.
*	Placeholder character for vestigial group password. Some systems use ! or x in this field. Linux uses group passwords.
GID	Group ID number.
adtl-members	List of group members in addition to those having the group in the GID field of their password file entry.

The HP-UX /etc/logingroup file

If present, this file has the sam syntax as */etc/group*. The user lists in this file determine each user's initial login group.

/etc/gshadow
The Linux shadow group file

name:pwd:group-admins:additional-users

name   Group names, as in */etc/group*.

pwd   Encoded group password, controls who can use the newgrp command with this group.

group-admins Group administrators: can change the group password and member lists.

adtl-users List of additional group members (usually the same as */etc/group*).

gpasswd

```
gpasswd group                      Change group password
gpasswd [options] user[,user…] group   Modify group files
```

Change password or add/remove group members and/or administrators.

Options

-a|-d   Add/remove users from *group*'s member list in both files.

-M   Specify the complete additional-members list (both files).

-A   Specify the complete group-administrator list.

-R|-r   Disable/remove group password, allowing no one/everyone to use newgrp with the group.

FreeBSD user classes

User classes allow account attributes and login environment settings to be applied to many accounts. Classes are independent of Unix groups. They are defined in */etc/login.conf*:

```
class-name:\
    :attribute=value:\
    :attribute=value:\
    ...
```

Important attributes are discussed in the next section.

cap_mkdb (FreeBSD)

    cap_mkdb -v *file*

Recreate the database that corresponds to *file* (often */etc/login.conf*).

Solaris Projects

projadd
projmod

    projadd [*options*] *name*
    projmod [*options*] *name*

Add or modify a project.

Options

-c *string*   Project description.

-p *n*   Set project ID to *n*.

-U *user*[,*user*]   Place user(s) into project.

-G *group*[,*group*] Place group(s) into project.

projdel

    projdel *name*

Remove a project.

projects

    projects -v [*user*]

List projects (or projects of which a user is a member), with descriptions.

newtask

    newtask -p *name*

Change current project to project *name*.

User Account Management Commands

useradd, usermod, userdel (HP-UX, Linux, Solaris)

```
useradd [options] username    Add a user account.
useradd -D options            Set new account defaults.
usermod options username      Modify a user account.
userdel [-r] username         Remove a user account.
```

These commands add, modify, and remove user accounts. useradd -D sets new default values for accounts subsequently created.

Options for useradd and usermod

-u *uid*   UID (defaults to the next highest unused UID).

-g *group*   Primary group.

-G *groups*   Comma-separated list of secondary groups.

-d *dir*   Full path to home directory (defaults to *current-base-dir/username*).

-s *shell*   Full path to login shell.

-c *full-name*
            Full name (user information field).

-m   Create home directory and copy standard initialization files to it.

-k *dir* (useradd *only*)
            Skeleton directory that contains default initialization files (*/etc/skel* is the default). This directory is valid only with -m.

-e *yyyy-mm-dd*
            Account expiration date (default is none).

-f *n*   Disable account if inactive for *n* days.

-p *encoded-pwd* (Linux)
            Encoded password (used when importing user accounts from another Unix system's password file).

-D (useradd *only*)

> Set defaults with -f, -e, -g, and -b (and -s under Linux).

-b *path* (useradd *only*)

> Base for home directories (valid only with -D).

adduser, chpass, rmuser (FreeBSD)

adduser [-s|-v]	*Add user account.*
chpass *user*	*Modify user account.*
rmuser *user*	*Remove user account.*

adduser adds a new user account via a series of prompts (some can also be set via options; see the man page). -s requests brief prompts, and -v requests verbose ones. chpass modifies the specified account via an editor session. rmuser removes the specified user account (also via prompts).

adduser defaults: /etc/adduser.conf

defaultpasswd = yes|no

> Whether to require passwords for user accounts.

dotdir = "*path*"

> Skeleton directory (defaults to */usr/share/skel*).

home = "*/path*"

> Home directory root (defaults to */home*).

defaultshell = "*name*"

> Login shell (defaults to tcsh)

defaultgroup = *group*|USER

> Default group. USER requests that a user-private group be created.

defaultclass = "*class-name*"

> Default user class (default is no assigned class).

uid_start = "*n*"

> Lowest UID assigned.

mkuser, chuser, rmuser (AIX)

```
mkuser attribute=value … user
chuser attribute=value … user
rmuser [-p] user
```

Create/modify/remove a user account. The -p option to rmuser removes the account stanzas from all configurations files, not just the password file.

User account attributes

See also page 44 for account expiration and pages 48–50 for password aging attributes.

id=*n*
> UID number.

prgp=*group*
> Primary group.

groups=*list*
> Group memberships (should include the primary group).

gecos="*full name*"
> User information password file field.

shell=*path*
> Login shell.

home=*path*
> Home directory.

login=true|false
> Whether local logins are allowed.

rlogin=true|false
> Whether remote logins are allowed.

daemon=true|false
> Whether user can use cron or the system resource controller.

logintimes=*list*
> Valid login times.

ttys=*list*
> Valid TTY locations.

loginretries=*n*
> Number of login failures after which to lock account.

expire=*MMDDhhmmYY*
> Account expiration date and time.

su=true|false
> Whether other users can su to this account.

sugroups=*list*
> Groups allowed to su to this account.

admin=true|false
> Whether account is an administrative account.

admgroups=*list*
> Groups that the account administers.

umask=*mask*
> Initial umask value.

User Account Attributes

Locking and unlocking a user account

AIX: chuser account_locked=true|false *user*.

FreeBSD: chpass -e *user* (use the account expiration date).

HP-UX: passwd -l *user* (to lock); edit */etc/passwd* to unlock.

Linux: passwd -l|-u *user*.

Solaris: passwd -l *user* (to lock); edit */etc/shadow* to unlock.

User account resource limits

AIX: */etc/security/limits*:
          cpu = *seconds*
          nofiles = *n*   *Number of open files*
          fsize, core, data, rss, stack *bytes*   *−1=no limit*

FreeBSD: */etc/login.conf*:
          :cputime=*seconds*:
          :maxproc=*n*:
          :openfiles=*n*:
          :priority=*nice#*:
          coredumpsize, datasize, filesize, memoryuse,
          memorylocked, sbsize, stacksize *bytes*|unlimited

System-wide initialization files

/etc/profile
> Bourne shell, Korn shell, and bash. Under Red Hat Linux, the scripts in */etc/profile.d* are also executed.

/etc/csh.cshrc, /etc/csh.login, and /etc/csh.logout
> Enhanced C shell (tcsh).

/etc/environment and /etc/security/environ (AIX)
> Additional sources of environment variable definitions.

/etc/login.conf (FreeBSD)
> The setenv entry sets environment variables for a class:
>
>   :setenv=VAR=value[,VAR=value...]:

/etc/login.defs (Linux)
> Users'/root paths are set via ENV_PATH and ENV_ROOTPATH.

User Authentication and Login Controls

Login message files

/etc/motd
> Message-of-the-day, displayed after a successful login.

/etc/issue
> Pre-login message (HP-UX, Linux, Solaris).

Login process controls

AIX:
  /etc/security/user:
  ```
  logintimes = ALL|time[,time]
  ```
  time is of the form [!][d[-d]]:start-end, where d is the day number (Monday=1). *start* and *end* are four-digit (24-hour) times. An initial ! functions as a negator.

`ttys = ALL|list`	*Omit "/dev".*
`loginretries = n`	*Lock account after n failures.*

  /etc/security/login.cfg:
  ```
  logintimes (as in /etc/security/user)
  ```

`logindisable = n`	*Disable port after n failures.*
`logininterval = seconds`	*Reset failure count.*
`logindelay = secs`	*Delay increase per attempt.*
`loginreenable = secs`	*Unlock locked port.*

FreeBSD: */etc/login.access*:
```
+|-:who:origins
```

The initial character, + or -, grants or denies access, respectively. *who* is a list of user and/or groups to whom the entry applies. *origins* is a list of TTYs, host names/addresses, domain names, and/or subnet addresses. Either list can include the keywords ALL, EXCEPT, and/or LOCAL.

/etc/login.conf:
```
:requirehome:                   Forbid login if home doesn't exist.
:times.allow|deny=time[,time...]:
```

time format: [*dd*[*dd...*]]*start-end*, where *dd* is a weekday (Mo, Tu, etc.). *start* and *end* are four-digit (24-hour) times.

`:ttys.xxx=list-of-names:`	*Omit "/dev."*
`:hosts.xxx=host-list:`	*Wildcards ok in list.*
`:yyytime=seconds:`	*Connect time limits.*

yyy can be day, week, month or session.

Linux: */etc/login.defs*:

`LOGIN_RETRIES n`	*Maximum login failures.*
`LOGIN_TIMEOUT secs`	*Delay between attempts.*
`DEFAULT_HOME yes|no`	*Allow login if home doesn't exist?*

Solaris: */etc/default/login*:

`TIMEOUT=secs`	*Login attempt timeout.*
`SLEEPTIME=secs`	*Delay between attempts.*
`SYSLOG=yes|no`	*Log root logins and all failures?*

Account expiration date

AIX: `chuser expires=MMDDhhwwYY`

FreeBSD: `chpass -e "mon day year"`; also, `expireperiod=nw|d` (days/weeks) in */etc/login.conf* (per user class)

Linux: `chage -E YYYY-MM-DD`

PAM

PAM is a freely available user authentication facility, currently provided by FreeBSD, HP-UX, Linux, and Solaris.

PAM configuration files: /etc/pam.d

Configuration files are named for the command to which they apply.* The other configuration provides defaults for PAM-aware services without their own configuration.

```
entry-type   result-action   module [args]
```

The various entry types are:

auth   Specifies procedures for user authentication.

account   Set user account attributes and apply account controls.

password   Used when a password change is required.

session   Configures logging to the syslog facility.

The group of entries of a particular type are processed in turn and form a *stack*. The aggregate results of all modules in the stack determine whether access is granted.

Result action keywords

sufficient
> Skip any remaining modules in the stack if this module grants access (return authentication success).

requisite
> If the module denies access, return authentication failure and skip any remaining modules in the stack.

required
> The module must grant access for authentication to succeed.

optional
> Results are used only when no other module is deterministic.

Important PAM modules

FreeBSD, HP-UX, and Solaris provide only a few PAM modules, but all modules are open source and can usually be built for these systems. Applicable stacks are in parentheses.

---

* An alternate configuration file, */etc/pam.conf*, can also be used, but the files in */etc/pam.d* take precedence.

pam_deny *(account, auth, passwd, session)*
pam_permit *(account, auth, passwd, session)*
> Always return failure and success, respectively. Stack either one with pam_warn for logging.

pam_warn *(account, auth, passwd, session)*
> Log information about the calling user and host to syslog.

pam_unix *(account, auth, passwd, session)*
> Verify (account), check aging for (account), or change (password) user passwords.* Important options are md5 (use MD5-encoded passwords), shadow (a shadow password file is in use), and try_first_pass (don't prompt for a password if another module has already done so).

pam_cracklib *(passwd)*
> Password triviality checking (stack with pam_unix). The module checks proposed passwords against the words in its dictionary file, */usr/lib/cracklib_dict,* and against the user's previous passwords stored in */etc/security/opasswd.*

> Other options include minlen=*n* (sets a minimum password length of *n*-1 using other default settings; see the man page) and difok=*n* (sets the number of characters in new password that must not be present in the old password, defaults to 10).

pam_limits *(session)*
> Sets user resource limits, as specified in */etc/security/limits.conf*:

>> *user-or-group*   hard|soft   *resource*   *limit-value*

> The most important resources are as (maximum address space), core (maximum core file size), cpu (CPU time, in minutes), fsize (maximum file size), nofile (maximum open files), data, and stack (maximum stack size). All sizes are expressed in kilobytes.

pam_listfile *(auth)*
> Allow or deny access based on items listed in an external file. Options include:

>> | | |
>> |---|---|
>> | sense=allow|deny | *Grant/deny access.* |
>> | file=*path* | *Location of file.* |
>> | item=*what* | *What the file contains.* |

> *what* is one of user, group, rhost, ruser, tty, or shell.

---

* There are also several other password checking modules. This is the most common.

---

pam_mkhomedir *(session)*
> Creates the user's home directory if it does not already exist, copying files from */etc/skel* to the new directory.

pam_nologin *(auth)*
> Prevents non-*root* logins if the file */etc/nologin* exists; the contents of the file are displayed to the user.

pam_rootok *(auth)*
> Allows *root* access without a password.

pam_securetty *(auth)*
> Limits *root* access to terminals listed in */etc/securetty*.

pam_time *(account)*
> Restricts access by time of day, based on user, group, tty, and/or shell, via the configuration in */etc/security/time.conf*:
>
> > `commands; ttys; users; times`
>
> Each field holds one or more items, joined with | (`OR`) or & (`AND`); ! indicates exclusion. *Times* syntax: `DDstart-end`; `DD` is one of Mo, Tu, We, Th, Fr, Sa, Su, Wk, Wd (weekday/end), or Al (all), and *start* and *end* are four-digit 24-hour times.
>
> Asterisks are wildcards (only one bare wildcard is allowed within the first three fields).

pam_wheel *(auth)*
> Designed for the su facility, this module denies *root* access to users who aren't members of a specified group. Options include:
>
> > group=*name*   *Applicable group (defaults to GID 0).*
> > deny   *Deny access.*

Solaris PAM modules

pam_projects *(account, auth, passwd, session)*
> Succeeds if the user belongs to a project and fails otherwise.

pam_dial_auth *(account, auth, passwd, session)*
> Authenticates dialup logins, using the configuration files */etc/dialup* and */etc/d_passwd* (see the following section).

pam_roles *(account, auth, passwd, session)*
> Autheticates role changes (see page 5).

Solaris and HP-UX dialup passwords

/etc/dialups
> Contains a list of special files that correspond to serial lines on which to accept dialup sessions.

/etc/d_passwd
> Per-shell dialup passwords. The entry format is as follows:
>
> ```
> shell-path:encoded-password:
> ```
>
> Under HP-UX, use passwd -F to modify this file:
>
> ```
> passwd -F /etc/d_passwd /shell-path
> ```

Password Selection and Aging

Password lifetimes

Minimum password lifetime

AIX:	chuser minage=*wks*	HP-UX:	passwd -n *days*
Linux:	chage -m *days*	Solaris:	passwd -n *days*

Maximum password lifetime

AIX:	chuser maxage=*wks*	HP-UX:	passwd -x *days*
Linux:	chage -M *days*	Solaris:	passwd -x *days*
FreeBSD:	passwordtime=*days*d in */etc/login.conf* (per class)		

Warning period (in advance of upcoming password expiration)

AIX:	chuser pwdwarntime=*days*		
HP-UX:	passwd -w *days*	Linux:	chage -W *days*
Solaris:	passwd -w *days*		
FreeBSD:	warnpassword=*days*d in */etc/login.conf* (user class)		

Inactivity period (before account is disabled after password expires)

AIX:	chuser maxexpired=*days*
Linux:	chage -I *days*

Set last password change date

FreeBSD:	chpass (interactive)
Linux:	chage -d *YYYY-MM-DD* (or local date format)

View current settings

AIX:	lsuser -f	HP-UX:	passwd -s
Linux:	chage -l	Solaris:	passwd -s

Default settings

AIX: In the default stanza of */etc/security/user*

FreeBSD: Settings for the appropriate user class in */etc/login.conf* (or the default class)

Linux: */etc/login.defs*:
          PASS_MAX_DAYS *days*
          PASS_MIN_DAYS *days*
          PASS_WARN_AGE *days*
          PASS_MIN_LEN *n*
          PASS_MAX_LEN *n*   *Encode only this many password characters.*

Solaris: */etc/default/passwd*:
          MAXWEEKS=*weeks*
          MINWEEKS=*weeks*
          WARNWEEKS=*weeks*
          PASSLENGTH=*n*   *Minimum password length.*

Password selection triviality checks

AIX account attributes

minalpha   Minimum number of alphabetic characters.

minother   Minimum number of nonalphabetic characters.

mindiff   Minimum number of characters not present in old password.

maxrepeats
           Maximum number of times any character can appear.

minlen   Actual minimum password length:

           minimum(minlen, minalpha+minother)

           Note that only the first 8 password characters are used.

dictionlist=*file*[,*file*]
           List of files that contain unacceptable passwords.

Linux

Configure via PAM modules (described previously in the "Important PAM modules" section).

FreeBSD: /etc/login.conf

`:minpasswordlen=n:`
Minimum password length.

`:passwd_format=md5:`
Use MD5 encoding (enables passwords > 8 characters).

`:mixpasswordcase=true:`
Disallow all lowercase passwords.

Password history lists

History lists prevent users from reselecting previous passwords.

AIX user account attributes

`histexpire=weeks`
Time until an old password can be reused (maximum is 260 weeks).

`histsize=n`
Number of old passwords to remember (maximum is 50).

HP-UX: /etc/default/security

`PASSWORD_HISTORY_DEPTH=n`
Remember n passwords (maximum is 10).

Forcing a password change

AIX:	`pwdadm -f ADMCHG`	FreeBSD:	`chpass` (interactive)
HP-UX:	`passwd -f`	Solaris:	`passwd -f`
Linux:	`chage -d 0` (add `-M 999` if not using aging)		

Process and Resource Management

Job control

command &
> Run the specified command in the background.

^Z   Stop foreground process.

jobs   List background processes.

fg [*job*] Resume the specified job in the foreground/background.
bg [*job*] *job* defaults to the stopped foreground job. %*n* refers to background job *n*. %?*str* refers to the background job whose command string contains the specified character string.

~^Z   Suspend an rlogin session. Add an additional tilde for each level of nesting (e.g., ~~^Z suspends a second-level rlogin session back to the first-level rlogin session, while ~^Z suspends the second-level session back to the local session).

---

ps   ps aux   *AIX, FreeBSD, Linux*
              /usr/ucb/ps aux   *Solaris*
              ps -elf   *System V version: HP-UX*

Display the detailed process list. The al option to the first two commands produces a different listing, which displays the process priority and nice number.

ps output columns

USER *(HP-UX:* UID)
> Username of the process owner

PID
> Process ID

%CPU
> Estimated fraction of CPU consumed (FreeBSD); CPU time/elapsed time (AIX, Solaris, Linux).

%MEM
> Estimated fraction of consumed system memory

SZ   Virtual memory used, in KB (HP-UX: pages)

RSS

> Physical memory used, in KB

TT *(HP-UX:* TTY)

> TTY associated with the process

STAT *(HP-UX:* S)

> Current process state flag(s):

> R Running or runnable
> S Sleeping
> I Idle (HP-UX: intermediate state)
> T Stopped
> Z Zombie process
> D Disk wait (not HP-UX)
> X Growing: waiting for memory (HP-UX)
> K Available kernel process (AIX)
> W Swapped out (not HP-UX)
> N Niced down (not HP-UX)
> < Niced: priority artificially raised (not HP-UX)

TIME

> Total CPU time used

COMMAND

> Command line being executed (truncated)

STARTED *(HP-UX:* STIME)

> Time or date the process started

F Flags associated with the process (see the ps manual page)

PPID

> Parent's PID

NI Process nice number

CP *(HP-UX:* C)

> Short term CPU-use factor; used by the scheduler for computing the execution priority (PRI)

PRI

> Actual execution priority (recomputed dynamically)

WCHAN

> Specifies the event the process is waiting for

kill   kill [-SIGNAL] pid(s)

Signal process(es). The default signal is TERM (terminate gently). Other useful signals are KILL (harsh kill), INTR (use with hung NFS processes), STOP, and CONT (halt and resume execution).

killall [-SIGNAL] pattern   *FreeBSD, Linux*

Kill all processes whose commands match the pattern.

---

renice   renice *m pid*   *Most systems*
         renice -n *m pid*   *AIX, HP-UX*
         priocntl -s -p *m* -i *pid proc-id*   *Solaris*

Change the nice number of the specified process to *m*.

---

vmstat   vmstat [*interval*] [*count*]

Display system performance statistics, refreshing the display every *interval* seconds, continuously, or a maximum of *count* times.

vmstat output columns

Column label variations are listed for each item.

r   Number of runnable processes.

b   Number of blocked processes (waiting for I/O).

w   Number of swapped-out runnable processes.

avm, act, swpd
    Number of active virtual-memory pages (snapshot).

fre, free
    Number of memory pages on the free list.

re Number of page reclaims.

pi, si, pin
    Number of pages that are paged-in (includes process startup).

po, so, pout
    Number of pages that are paged-out.

fr Memory pages that have been freed by the virtual-memory management facility during the interval.

dn Disk operations per second on disk *n*. Not all versions of vmstat include disk data.

cs Number of context switches.

us Percentage of total CPU time spent on user processes.

sy Percentage of total CPU time spent on system overhead.

id Idle time percentage (unused CPU time).

Display amount of physical memory

> AIX: lsattr -HE -l sys0 -a realmem
> FreeBSD: grep memory /var/run/dmesg.boot
> HP-UX: dmesg | grep Phys   Linux: free
> Solaris: dmesg | grep mem

iostat

iostat [*refresh-interval*]

Display I/O statistics (not available for Linux).

sar

sar [*options*] *interval* [*count*]

Display system performance statistics (not available for FreeBSD). The most useful option is -d, which displays disk statistics. Its other capabilities are performed better by vmstat.

sa

sa [-m] [*options*]

By default, displays image-based accounting data, summarized by command/program. Use -m to produce a user-based report instead.

Output suffix labels (option to sort on this item, if any)

no suffix (-n)
  Number of times called

cp, cpu   CPU time (system + user), in minutes

re	Elapsed time, in minutes
avio *(-d)*	Average number of I/O operations per execution
k *(-k)*	CPU time-averaged memory use in KB
k*sec *(-K)*	Aggregate memory use, in KB-seconds
tio *(-D)*	Total I/O operations for all executions
s	System CPU time, in minutes
u	User CPU time, in minutes

Other options

-b	Sort by average CPU time/execution.
-r	Reverse sort order.
-l	Separate system and user time in the report.
-f -v *n*	Limit report to commands executed at least n times.
-c	Show times as percentages rather than as raw values.

---

ac ac [*options*] [*user(s)*]

Show total connect-time data for all users or the specified user(s).

Options

-p Subtotal by user.

-d Subtotal by date.

The cron Facility

File locations

crontab file

Usual: */var/spool/cron/crontabs*
FreeBSD: */var/spool/cron*

Linux: /var/spool/cron (Red Hat), /var/spool/cron/tabs (SuSE)
FreeBSD and Linux also use the additional file /etc/crontab.

cron.allow and cron.deny files

Usual: /var/adm/cron
FreeBSD: /var/cron
Linux: /etc (Red Hat), /var/spool/cron (SuSE)
Solaris: /etc/cron.d

cron log file

Usual: /var/adm/cron/log
FreeBSD: /var/log/cron
Linux: /var/log/cron (Red Hat); not configured (SuSE)
Solaris: /var/cron/log

cron subsystem configuration

FreeBSD: /etc/rc.conf: cron_enable="yes|no" and cron_flags="args"
HP-UX: /etc/rc.config.d/cron: CRON="YES|NO"
Linux: /etc/cron.* directories hold scripts for cron to run.
Solaris: /etc/default/cron: CRONLOG="log-path"

---

crontab   crontab [options] [-u user] [file]

Installs the current or specified user's *crontab* file.

Options (filename not allowed)

-e   Edit the current file.

-l   List current *crontab* entries.

-r   Remove all current entries.

---

cronttab file format

    mins hrs day-of-month month weekday cmd   *Most systems*
    mins hrs day-of-month month weekday user cmd *FreeBSD*

The various fields are explained here. Note that fields
can hold a single value, a comma-separated list of values,
a range of values (e.g., 1-4), or a wildcard.

mins   Minutes after the hour: 0-59.

hrs   Hour of the day: 0-23 (0=midnight).

---

day-of-month
>   Numeric day within a month: 1-31.

month   The month of the year: 1-12.

weekday   The day of the week: 0-6 (0=Sunday). In the BSD format, Sunday is 7 (Monday is 1 in both schemes).

cmd   Command to run.

user   User account to run the command (BSD format only).

*   Wildcard character for the first five fields.

%   Inserts a new line character into the command string.

Linux and FreeBSD enhancements to the crontab format

- Months and days of the week may be specified as names, abbreviated to their first three letters: sun, mon, jan, feb, etc.

- Sunday can be specified as either 0 or 7.

- Ranges and lists can be combined (e.g., 2,4,6-7 is a legal entry). HP-UX also supports this enhancement.

- Step values can be specified with a /n suffix (e.g., the hours entry 8-18/2 means "every 2 hours from 8 a.m. to 6 p.m.," and the minutes entry */5 means "every 5 minutes").

- Environment variables can be defined within the *crontab* file using the usual Bourne shell syntax (e.g., MAILTO may be used to specify a user to receive mail messages). Other environment variables include SHELL, PATH, and HOME.

- On FreeBSD systems, special strings may be used to replace the scheduling fields entirely:

    @reboot: Run at system reboots.
    @yearly: Run at midnight on January 1.
    @monthly: Run at midnight on the first of every month.
    @weekly: Run at midnight every Sunday.

@daily:	Run at midnight every day.
@hourly:	Run on the hour, every hour, every day.

cron.allow and cron.deny files

Both files hold lists of usernames, one username per line. The contents of these files determine who can run the crontab command, and they are interpreted as follows:

- If *cron.allow* exists, a user's username must be listed within it for the user to run crontab.

- If *cron.allow* does not exist, but *cron.deny* does exist, any user not listed in *cron.deny* may use the crontab command. *cron.deny* may be empty to allow unlimited access to the crontab command.

- If neither file exists, only *root* can use crontab, except under Linux and FreeBSD, in which the default build configuration of cron allows everyone to use it.

Note that these files do not affect any existing *crontab* entries (which will continue to be executed until they are removed).

Managing Paging Space

View paging spaces list and usage

AIX:	`lsps -a`	FreeBSD:	`pstat -s`
HP-UX:	`swapinfo -t -a -m`	Solaris:	`swap -l`
Linux:	`cat /proc/swaps` (list), `free -m -o` (usage)		

pagesize (FreeBSD, AIX, Solaris)

`pagesize`

Display the size of a memory page.

Defining paging areas

Place swap in the filesystem type field of */etc/fstab* (Solaris: */etc/vfstab*):

FreeBSD:	*device*	none	swap	sw	0 0
HP-UX:	*device*	…	swap	pri=n	0 0

Linux:	*device* swap swap defaults 0 0	
Solaris:	*device* - - swap - no -	
AIX:	List in /etc/swapspaces:	
	name:	*Identifying label*
	dev = *device*	*Logical volume special file*

---

swapon swapon -a

Activate all configured paging spaces.

Adding a filesystem paging area

AIX:	mkps -a -n -s *#partitions vgname*
FreeBSD:	dd if=/dev/zero of=/*path* bs=1024 count=*n*
	vnconfig -e vn*nc* /*path* swap
HP-UX:	swapon [-m *min-size*] [-l *max-size*] [-r *reserve*] *dir*
	reserve is the amount of space that must always remain in the filesystem (in blocks).
Linux:	dd if=/dev/zero of=/*path* bs=1024 count=*n*
	mkswap /*path* *n*
	sync; sync
	swapon /*path*
Solaris:	mkfile *n*m /*path* *m means MB.*
	swap -a /*path* 0 *size-in-blocks*

Filesystems and Disks

Filesystem Configuration File

/etc/fstab

location mount-dir fs-type dump-freq fsck-pass options

Filesystem configuration file.

special-file
   Filesystem location. For traditional local filesystems, this is
   the partition's block special file. A logical volume may also be
   specified if an LVM is in use. For NFS remote filesystems, the
   format is *host*:/*path*.

For Samba filesystems, the Linux format is *//host/share*. The
FreeBSD format is *//user@host/share*.

mount-dir
   Directory where the filesystem will be mounted.

fs-type
   Filesystem type keyword.

dump-freq
   Integer indicating the frequency this filesystem should be
   backed up by the dump utility.

fsck-pass
   Integer indicating the order fsck should check filesystems.

options
   Comma-separated list of options or the keyword defaults.

/etc/vfstab (Solaris)

block-dev char-dev mt-dir fs-type fsck-pass auto? opts

Similar syntax to the tradition *fstab* file, except:

- Both block (for mounting) and character (for fcsk) special
  files are listed as the first two fields.
- *auto?* is either yes or no, depending on whether the filesystem
  should be mounted automatically at boot time with mount -a.
- The dump frequency field is not included.

/etc/filesystems (AIX)

```
mount-pt:
  attribute = value
  …
```

Attributes

dev = /dev/*logical-volume*
   Logical volume.

vol = "*name*"
   Descriptive label.

```
vfs = jfs2
```
Filesystem type: jfs2 for local, nfs for NFS.

```
log = /dev/log-vol
```
Device to use for filesystem log.

```
mount = true|false
```
Mount automatically?

```
check = n
```
Sets the fsck pass.

```
options = list
```
Mount options.

```
quota = keywords
```
userquota and groupquota enable user and group disk quotas.

Filesystem types

Local

AIX:	jfs2	FreeBSD:	ufs
HP-UX:	vxfs, hfs	Linux:	ext2, ext3, reiserfs
Solaris:	ufs		

CD-ROM

AIX:	cdrfs	FreeBSD:	cd9660
HP-UX:	cdfs	Linux:	iso9660
Solaris:	hsfs		

DOS

FreeBSD:	msdos	Linux:	msdos
Solaris:	pcfs		

Samba

FreeBSD:	smbfs	Linux:	smbfs

Filesystem mounting options

Used within the filesystem configuration file and by the mount command.

rw	Read/write filesystem (default for read/write devices).
ro	Read-only filesystem (default for read-only media).

[no]suid   Whether SetUID access mode is honored (default: suid).

[no]auto   Whether to automatically mount this filesystem at boot time; auto is the default (Linux, FreeBSD).

[no]exec   Whether to allow binary programs to execute; exec is the default (Linux, FreeBSD).

[no]dev   Whether to allow device access via special files; dev is the default (AIX, Linux, FreeBSD).

user   Allow ordinary users to mount this filesystem (Linux).

[no]grpid   Whether to use BSD-style group ownership inheritance (directory's group owner) or System V-style (owner's primary group); BSD-style is the default (Linux).

resuid=*n*   Set the UID/GID, which has access to the reserved
resgid=*n*   blocks with the filesystem (Linux ext2/ext3).

largefiles

     Support files > 2 GB (HP-UX VxFS, Solaris).

[no]logging

     Whether to maintain a transaction log (Solaris). The default is nologging.

nolog   Don't use a transaction log (HP-UX VxFS).

delaylog   Delay writing log entries slightly to improve performance, increasing risk of loss slightly. (HP-UX VxFS)

writeback   Write out log metadata and filesystem blocks in either order, for a slight performance improvement and increased risk of loss in the event of a crash (Linux ext3).

forcedirectio

     Use direct I/O to this filesystem (i.e., no buffering); this is useful for applications such as databases.

notail   Disable default behavior of storing small files directly within the hash tree (Linux ReiserFS).

resize=*n*   Resize the filesystem to *n* blocks upon mounting (Linux ReiserFS).

quota   Enable disk quotas (HP-UX, Solaris).

userquota *and* groupquota
             Enable user/group disk quotas (FreeBSD).

usrquota *and* grpquota
             Enable user/group disk quotas (Linux).

pri=*n*   Set swap space priority (0 to 32767). Under Linux, higher numbers indicate more favored areas, which are used first; HP-UX favors lower priority areas.

Additional mount options for NFS filesystems

bg   If the NFS mount of this filesystem fails on the first try, continue retrying in the background (speeds up booting when remote filesystems are unavailable).

retry=*n*   Retry mount *n* times before giving up (default is 100000).

timeo=*n*   Set the timeout—the length of time to wait for the first try of each individual NFS request before giving up—to the specified number of tenths of seconds. Each subsequent retry doubles the previous timeout value.

retrans=*n* Retransmit a request *n* times before giving up (default is 3).

soft, hard   Quit/continue trying to connect, even after the retrans value is met. soft should be used only with read-only filesystems.

intr   Allow an interrupt to kill a hung process (recommended with hard).

rsize=*n*   Specify the size of the read or write buffer in bytes.
wsize=*n*

Filesystem-Related Commands

df   df -k [*file-system*]

             Display the status of the specified filesystem or all mounted filesystems (sizes are in KB).

du   du -k [-s] *directories*

Display disk space consumption for each subdirectory in the specified directory tree(s), in KB. -s says to display only the total for each listed directory.

---

quot   quot *file-system*

Display total disk usage for each user within the specified filesystem (not available for Linux).

---

fsck   fsck [*options*] *device*

Options

-p (-o p *under Solaris*)
  Preen the filesystem; automatically perform repairs that don't change the contents of any file.

-n Answer "no" to all prompts; list, but don't repair, any problems found.

-y Answer "yes" to all prompts; repair all damage, regardless of severity. Use this option with caution.

-b *n*
  Use an alternate superblock located at block *n*.

---

fuser fuser [*options*] *device|file*

Report on open files within the specified filesystem or on the status of the specified file.

Options

-u Include the user who owns each process in the display.

-k Kill all of the processes associated with the open files.

---

mount mount [*options*] *file-system mount-point*

Mount the specified filesystem at *mount-point*.

Options

-t *type* Specify filesystem type. AIX uses -v, and Solaris uses -F for this option. Local filesystem types are listed on page 61. NFS filesystems are type nfs.

-a Mount all filesystems in the filesystem configuration file, allowing automatic mounts.

-o *fs-options*

    Pass filesystem type-specific options to its mount command.

---

umount umount [*options*] [*file-system*]

Unmount the specified filesystem(s).

Options

-a [-t *type*]

    Unmount all mounted filesystems (or all of the specified type). AIX uses -v, and Solaris uses -F for this option. FreeBSD and Linux also allow the *type* keyword to be preceded with no (e.g., nonfs).

-f Force the unmount operation, even if there are items in use.

-h *host (FreeBSD and Solaris)*

    Unmount all remote filesystems from the specified host.

---

mknod mknod *name* c|b *major minor*

Create a device special file. c or b selects a character or block special file. The final arguments are the major and minor device numbers for the device.

MAKEDEV

cd /dev; ./MAKEDEV *device-name*   *Omit "/dev"*

Script to create special files associated with the specified device. Not available on all systems.

---

mkfs	newfs [options] device	FreeBSD, HP-UX, Solaris
newfs	mkfs [options] device	Linux

Create a filesystem on device.

Options

-t ext2|ext3 *(Linux)*
-F hfs|vxfs *(HP-UX)*
    Select filesystem type.

-b *bsize*
    Filesystem block size in bytes (must be a power of 2). Defaults are:

        FreeBSD: 16384   Linux: 1024
        Solaris: 8192
        HP-UX: 1024–8192 (depends on filesystem size)

-f *fsize*
    Filesystem fragment size: the smallest allocatable unit of disk space (typically, *bsize*/8). Defaults:

        FreeBSD: 2048   Linux: not available
        HP-UX: 1024   Solaris: 1024

-i *bpi*
    Number of bytes per inode (i.e., #inodes created= total-size / *bpi*). Defaults:

        FreeBSD: 8192 (or 4*fsize) Linux: 4096
        HP-UX: 6144   Solaris: 2048

-m *free*
    Percentage of free space reserved for *root*. Defaults:

        FreeBSD: 8%   Linux: 5%
        HP-UX: 10%   Solaris: 10%

-U *(FreeBSD)*
    Enable soft updates (recommended).

-o speed | space *(FreeBSD)*
    Set the optimization preference. speed means that the filesystem will attempt to minimize the time spent allocating disk blocks, while space means that it will try to minimize disk fragmentation. The

default is space if the minimum free space percentage is less than 8%; otherwise, the default is speed.

-l *(HP-UX)*
Enable files larger than 2 GB.

-j [-J *device*] *(Linux ext3)*
Enable journalling and, optionally, specify a separate log device. Convert an existing ext2 filesystem to ext3 with tune2fs -j *device*.

mkreiserfs (Linux)

    mkreiserfs [options] device

Create a Reiser filesystem on device.

Options

-j *device*
Specify the journal device.

-s *blocks*
Specify the journal size.

crfs (AIX)

    crfs -v jfs2 -g vgname|-d lvname -m mt-pt [options]

Create a filesystem in the specified volume group.

Options

-g *vgname*
Create the filesystem on a new logical volume in this volume group.

-d *lvname*
Use this existing logical volume.

-m *mt-pt*
Mount a point for the filesystem.

-A yes|no
Whether the filesystem is mounted at boot time by mount -a commands.

-a size=*n*
Size of the filesystem, in 512-byte blocks.

```
-a frag=n
    Use a fragment size of n bytes (default is 4096).

-a nbpi=n
    Number of bytes per inode (default is 4096).

-l device
    Specify the logging logical volume.
```

Increasing the size of an existing filesystem

Enlarge the partition/logical volume first. The new size usually
defaults to the full size of the underlying device. The *size* units are
usually blocks (Linux ReiserFS uses bytes).

```
AIX:       chfs [-a size=[+]size]
FreeBSD:   growfs device [size]
Linux:     resize2fs device [size]        (ext2/ext3)
           resize_reiserfs [-s [+]size]   (Reiser)
```

Adding a New Disk

The summaries in this section assume that the disk has already
been installed in the system. It was not possible to include all of
the commands mentioned below in this reference.

AIX (using LVM)

1. Use cfgmgr to identify the new disk (if necessary).
2. Add the disk to a volume group (mkvg or extendvg). Activate
   any new volume group (varyonvg).
3. Create/enlarge logical volumes (mklv or extendlv).
4. Create filesystems (crfs).
5. Run fsck.

FreeBSD

1. Divide the disk into slices/physical partitions (fdisk).
2. Create special files for slices other than the first (mknod).
3. Create FreeBSD partitions within each slice (disklabel).
4. Create a filesystem (newfs).
5. Run fsck on the new filesystem.

HP-UX (using LVM)

1. Designate the disk as a physical volume (pvcreate).
2. Place the disk into a new or existing volume group (vgcreate or vgextend). For a new volume group, create a subdirectory in /dev and the associated special file for the new volume group prior to running vgcreate.
3. Create logical volumes (lvcreate).
4. Run lvlnboot on *root* and swap logical volumes.
5. Build a filesystem (newfs).
6. Run fsck.

Linux

1. If necessary, create the special files for the disk (MAKEDEV).
2. Divide the disk into partitions (fdisk or other). Set partition types appropriately: 82 for a Linux swap partition, and 83 for a regular Linux partition.
3. Create a new filesystem (mkfs or mkreiserfs).
4. Run fsck -f or reiserfsck on the new filesystem.

Solaris

1. Write a generic disk label (format, label subcommand).
2. Divide the disk into partitions (format, partition subcommand). Save the updated disk label (label subcommand).
3. Create filesystems (newfs).
4. Run fsck.

Display disk list/data

AIX:	lspv		
FreeBSD:	egrep "[sh]d" `dmesg`		
HP-UX:	ioscan -f -n -C disk		
Linux:	fdisk -l	Solaris:	getdev

Logical Volume Managers

Terminology variations

logical volume manager (LVM)

FreeBSD: Vinum Volume Manager
Solaris: Volume Manager

volume group

FreeBSD: n/a   Solaris: volume

logical volume (holds filesystem)

FreeBSD: volume   Solaris: n/a

extent (disk space allocation unit)

AIX: partition   FreeBSD: subdisk

Special files used to build filesystems

AIX: /dev/*lvname*   FreeBSD: /dev/vinum/*lvname*
Solaris: /dev/md/[r]dsk/*dn*   HP-UX, Linux: /dev/vgname/*lvname*

Vendor-specific preparatory steps

Initialize the volume manager (Solaris)

```
metadb -a -f slice-name          Create initial state database replicas.
metadb -a -c 2 slice-name        Add a replica on this slice.
```

Designate a disk as a physical volume (HP-UX and Linux)

HP-UX: pvcreate *disks*   Linux: pvcreate *disks*

Set partition type (Linux)

Partitions must have the type set to 8E (use fdisk).

Volume group commands

Create a volume group

```
AIX:           mkvg -y vgname disks
HP-UX, Linux:  vgcreate vg-dev disk(s)
Solaris:       metainit dn n 1 slice-name1 … 1 slicenamen
```

Add disk to existing volume group

AIX:	extendvg *vgname disk*
HP-UX, Linux:	vgextend *vg-dev disk(s)*
Solaris:	metainit *dn* 1 1 *slice-name1*

Remove disk from volume group

AIX:	reducevg *vgname disk*
HP-UX, Linux:	vgreduce *vg-dev disk*

Remove entire volume group

AIX:	Remove all disks with reducevg
HP-UX, Linux:	vgremove *vg-dev*
Solaris:	metaclear /dev/md/dsk/*dn*

Logical volume commands

Create a logical volume

AIX:	mklv -y *lvname vgname #logical-partitions*
HP-UX, Linux:	lvcreate -n *lvname* -L *size-in-MB vg-name*

Increase logical volume size

AIX:	extendlv *lvname #logical-partitions*
HP-UX, Linux:	lvextend -L *size-in-MB lv-dev*

Remove a logical volume

AIX:	rmlv *lvname*
HP-UX, Linux:	lvremove *lv-dev*

Displaying LVM information

List all volume groups/volumes

AIX:	lsvg	FreeBSD:	vinum *lv*
Linux:	vgdisplay -s	Solaris:	metastat
HP-UX:	vgdisplay | grep "VG N"		

List logical volumes/plexes in a volume group/volume

AIX:	lsvg -l *vgname*	FreeBSD:	vinum lp
HP-UX, Linux:	vgdisplay -v *vgname*		

List volume group's/volume's component disks

AIX: `lsvg -p` *vgname*   FreeBSD: `vinum ls -v`
HP-UX, Linux: `vgdisplay -v` *vgname*
Solaris: `metastat` *dn*

Display volume group/volume attributes

AIX: `lsvg` *vgname*
FreeBSD: `vinum lv -V` *vol-name*
HP-UX, Linux: `vgdisplay` *vgname*
Solaris: `metaparam` *dn*

List disks on which a logical volume/plex resides

AIX: `lslv -l` *lvname*
FreeBSD: `vinum lp -V` *plex-name*
HP-UX: `lvdisplay -v` *lv-dev* `| head -25`
Linux: `lvdisplay -d` *lvname*

Display logical volume/plex attributes

AIX: `lslv` *lvname*
FreeBSD: `vinum lp -V` *plex-name*
HP-UX, Linux: `lvdisplay` *lv-dev*

Disk mirroring

AIX: `mklv -y` *lvname* `-c` *#copies vgname #phys-parts*
FreeBSD: `volume mirror` (description file)
HP-UX: `lvcreate -m` *#copies* `-s` *g* `-n` *lvname* `-L` *MB vg*
Linux: `raid-level 1` (*/etc/raidtab*)
Solaris: `metainit` *dn* `-m` *dnmirror1*
           `metaattach` *dn dnmirror2*

Software disk striping

AIX: `mklv -S` *stripe-size*`K` *vgname #phys-partitions*
FreeBSD: `plex org striped` (description file)
HP-UX: `lvcreate -i` *#stripes* `[-I` *KB*`] -n` *lv* `-L` *MB vg-dev*
Linux: `raid-level 0` (*/etc/raidtab*)
Solaris: `metainit` *dn* `1` *n slice-name1* … *slice-namen*

Software RAID 5 volumes

FreeBSD:	plex org raid5 (description file)
Linux:	raid-level 5 (*/etc/raidtab*)
Solaris:	metainit *dn* -r *slice-names* -i *slicek*

The FreeBSD vinum volume manager

vinum create *description-file*
  Create entities defined in the specified description file.

vinum init *volume.plex*
  Initialize the subdisks in the specified plex.

vinum start *volume.plex*
  Create/regenerate a mirror.

Description file format

```
drive d1 device /dev/disk                          Define drives.
drive d2 device /dev/disk
...

volume name
  plex org concat|striped|raid5 [stripe-sizeK]     Plex type.
    sd length km drive dn                          List of drives.
    ...
volume mirror name
  plex org concat                                  First mirror.
    sd length km drive dn
  plex org concat                                  Second mirror.
    sd length km drive dn
```

Configuring Linux md devices: /etc/raidtab

```
raiddev /dev/mdj                    Define RAID device j (starts at 0).
raid-level lev                      RAID level.
nr-raid-disks n                     Number of component disks.
[chunk-size KB]                     Stripe size.
persistent-superblock 1            Enable boot autostarting.
device /dev/disk                    First component disk.
raid-disk 0                         Number the disk.
...                                 Repeat for all component disks.
```

Sharing Local Filesystems with NFS

/etc/exports

```
pathname -option,option...            AIX, FreeBSD, HP-UX
pathname host(options) host(options)             Linux
```

List filesystems to be exported.

Options

Host lists are separated by colons in applicable options.
Note that the Linux file format does not use hosts lists.

rw=*list*
ro=*list*

Read/write and read-only access lists. rw is the default.

root=*list*
> Hosts where *root* status may be retained for this
> filesystem.

anon=*n*
maproot=*n* *(FreeBSD)*
> Map remote root access to the specified UID.

mapall=*n* *(FreeBSD)*
> Map all remote users to the specified UID.

root_squas*h*
> Map UID 0 and GID 0 values to the anonymous
> values (under Linux, map values to those specified
> in the anonuid and anongid options). This is the
> default.

anonuid=*n and* anongid=*n* *(Linux)*
> UID/GID to which to map incoming *root*/group 0
> access.

noaccess *(Linux)*
> Prohibits access to the specified directory and its
> subdirectories. This option is used to prevent access
> to part of a tree that has already been exported.

[no]secure *(Linux)*
> Whether to require NFS access to be via the normal
> privileged NFS port. secure is the default.

/etc/dfs/dfstab (Solaris)

```
share -F nfs -o option-list pathname
```

List filesystems to be exported. Options are the same as those listed in */etc/experts*.

exportfs

```
exportfs -a                              Most systems
kill -HUP `cat /var/run/mountd.pid`      FreeBSD
```

Export all filesystems in */etc/exports* (or */etc/dfs/dfstab*).

showmount

```
showmount -e|-a
```

List exported filesystems (-e) or hosts that have remotely mounted any local filesystems (-a).

Backups

dump
```
dump options filesystem
dump option-letters option-args filesystem        HP-UX,
                                                  Solaris
```

Perform a backup of the specified filesystem, based on the option settings. The second (older) form does not use hyphens before option letters, and it places arguments after the option string:

```
dump abc a-arg b-arg c-arg …
```

Correct argument ordering is thus imperative.

Command name

AIX:	backup	FreeBSD:	dump
HP-UX:	dump, vxdump	Solaris:	ufsdump
Linux:	dump (ext2/ext3 only)		

Options

-0, …, -9 Dump level (0 = full backup; 1–9 are incremental levels).

-u   Update the history file (*/etc/dumpdates*) after
            completing the backup. This file must be
            created with touch before dump is used.

-f *device*

            Write the backup to the specified device
            (- means standard output).

-W   Preview the backup operation, but don't do
            anything.

-s *feet* -d *dens*

            Traditionally, these options were needed to
            determine the capacity of the backup media
            (capacity = *feet* * *dens*). Recent versions of dump
            generally don't need them, because these
            versions keep writing until they detect an end-
            of-media mark.

-b *factor*

            Specify the block size to use on the tape in
            units of 1024 (or sometimes 512) bytes.

fbackup (HP-UX)

fbackup *dump-options* [-i *path*] [-e *path*] ...

Perform a backup of the files and directories specified to
-i, excluding ones given to -e; both options may be used
more than once. You can also specify what to include/
exclude in a graph file (specify with -g), which has
entries of the form:

    i|e *path*

restore   restore *options* [*items*]
              restore *option-letters* *option-args* [*items*]   HP-UX,
                                                                         Solaris

Restore items from a dump archive.

Options

-r   Read and restore the entire tape.

-x	Extract listed files and directories, restoring them in the current directory. Filenames are relative to the root directory of the filesystem being restored (i.e., mount point is removed: *pub/gold.dat* not */chem/pub/gold.dat*).
-t	Type the names of the listed files and directories if they appear on the backup tape (or all files on the tape, if none are specified). Useful for creating a table of contents.
-f *file*	Name of the file or device holding the dump (- means standard input).
-s *n*	Use the *n*th tape file for the restore (the default is 1).
-I	Enter interactive mode. Subcommands include cd (change directory within the archive), ls (list files), add *file* (add file to the extraction list), delete *file* (remove file from the extraction list), extract (perform the restore), and quit.

frecover (HP-UX)

frecover *restore-options* [-i *path*] [-e *path*] ...

-i and -e indicate items to include/exclude from the restore operation, and -g may be used to specify a graph file (as with fbackup).

Additional options

-X Restore files relative to the current directory (converting absolute pathnames to relative ones).

-F Restore files into the current directory, stripping off all paths.

-o Overwrite files on disk that are newer than the file in the backup set.

-N List archive files without performing a restore (useful for creating a table of contents).

dd   dd [option=value …]

Perform raw tape I/O.

Options

if=file|device
   Source for input data.

of=file|device
   Output file: destination for data.

ibs=bytes
   Input block size (the default is 512).

obs=bytes
   Output block size (the default is 512).

fskip=n
   Skip n tape files before transferring data (not available in all implementations).

count=c
   The amount of data (number of blocks) to transfer.

conv=keys
   Keyword(s) that specify the desired conversion of input data before outputting; swab means "swap bytes," and it is the most commonly used conversion type. lcase and ucase mean "convert to lower/upper case," and ascii and ebcdic mean "convert to ASCII or EBCDIC."

mt   mt [-f tape-device] subcommand

Manipulate tapes and tape devices. *tape-device* specifies which tape drive to use, and *subcommand* is a keyword that indicates the desired action.

Subcommands

rewind   Rewind the tape.

status   Display device status (e.g., in use).

fsf n   Skip the next n tape files.

bsf n   Skip back n tape files.

Backing up the system filesystem

AIX: `mksysb -i `*`tape-device`*
HP-UX: `make_recovery -r -A -d `*`tape-device`*` -C`

Creating rescue floppies

Mount the first installation CD before beginning.

FreeBSD: `dd if=/`*`dir`*`/floppies/fixit of=/dev/rfd0c bs=36b`
Linux: `dd if=/`*`dir`*`/disks/rescue of=/dev/fd0 bs=18k`

Printing

Printing subsystem components

Spool directories

AIX: */var/spool/lpd/qdir* and */var/spool/qdaemon*
FreeBSD: */var/spool/output/lpd/**
HP-UX: */var/spool/lp/request/**
Linux: */var/spool/lpd/**
Solaris: */var/spool/lp/requests/**

Configuration file(s)

AIX: */etc/qconfig*   FreeBSD: */etc/printcap*
HP-UX: */etc/lp/**   Linux: */etc/printcap*
Solaris: */etc/lp/** and */etc/printers.conf*

Boot script configuration

FreeBSD: */etc/rc.conf*: `lpd_enable="YES"`
HP-UX: */etc/rc.config.d/lp*: `LP=1`
SuSE Linux: */etc/sysconfig/printer*: `DEFAULT_PRINTER=`*`name`*

The BSD and LPRng Spooling Subsystems

Used by FreeBSD and some Linux systems.

lpq	`lpq [-P `*`printer`*`	-a]`

     List the contents of the default queue (no options), specified queue, or all queues.

lprm   lprm [-P *printer*] *list*

Remove print jobs from a queue. *list* can contain print-job IDs and/or usernames (remove all jobs owned by the specified user); if *list* is a single hyphen, all jobs are removed from the specified queue.

---

lpc   lpc [*subcommand args*]

Administrative utility. Executes the specified *subcommand*, or enters interactive mode if no *subcommand* is specified.

Subcommands

status *printer*
    Display status of the line printer daemon and the specified print queue.

start *printer*
    Restart printing on the printer after an abort or stop command.

stop *printer*
    Stop all printing on printer after the current job has finished (new jobs are still accepted).

abort *printer*
    Stop all printing on printer immediately (new jobs are still accepted).

clean *printer*
    Remove all jobs from the printer's queue. The current job will still complete.

disable *printer*
    Prevent users from adding new jobs to the specified queue (printing continues).

enable *printer*
    Allow users to spool jobs to the queue.

down *printer*
    Stop printing and disable the queue for *printer* (disable plus stop).

---

up *printer*
> Enable the queue and start printing on *printer* (enable plus start).

topq *printer job-ID*
> Move the specified job to the top of the queue.

LPRng enhancements to lpc

hold *queue* [*ids*]
> Place the specified job, or all jobs in the queue, into a hold state, preventing them from printing.

release *queue* [*ids*]
> Allow the specified held print job(s) to print.

holdall *queue*
> Place all new jobs entering the queue into the held state. Use noholdall to terminate this behavior (held jobs will still need to be released explicitly).

move *old-queue ids new-queue*
> Transfer the specified print jobs between queues.

redirect *old-queue new-queue*
> Redirect jobs from the old queue to the new queue. Specify off as the new queue to turn off redirection.

redo *queue* [*id*]
> Reprint the specified job.

kill *queue*
> Kill the current job, and then restart the queue. This option is equivalent to abort plus start.

active *printer*[*@host*]
> Determine whether the specified spool daemon is active.

reread *printer*[*@host*]
> Force the specified spool daemon to reread its configuration files.

class *queue class-list*
> Limit printing from the specified queue to jobs in the specified class(es), where *class-list* is usually a comma-separated list of one or more class letters. The keyword off removes any current class restrictions in effect.

/etc/printcap configuration file

```
name[|name|name…]:\
  :xx=|#value:yy[@]:\
  …
```

xx is an attribute name, and *value* is its setting. Attribute definitions are enclosed in colons, and each line within an entry ends with a backslash.

The assignment character varies by data type: = for strings, # for numeric, and @ or nothing (no value) for Boolean off/on.

printcap fields

br#*nnnn* Baud rate for serial line printers.

mc#*copies* Maximum number of copies that can be requested (FreeBSD only).

mj#*jobs* Maximum number of jobs in queue (not available under FreeBSD or some versions of Linux).

mx#*size* Maximum file size (0 = no limit).

pc#*price* Price per page/foot (units = $0.0001).

pl#*lines* Page length, in lines.
pw#*rows* Page width, in characters.

px#*pixels* Page width, in pixels.
py#*pixels* Page length, in pixels.

rg=*group* Restrict printing to members of the specified group (not always implemented).

rw[@] Open output device read-write.

hl[@] Create a printer burst page after each job.

sb[@] Use a one-line banner only.

sc[@] Suppress multiple copy requests.

sf[@] Suppress form feeds.

sh[@] Suppress burst (header) pages.

*x*f=*path* Filters, where the initial character defines the filter type: if=input and accounting, of=general output,

---

cf=cifplot, df=dvi/TEX, ff=Fortran (form feed), gf=plot, nf=ditroff, tf=troff, vf=raster image, xf=pass-through (for preformatted output).

af=*path*   Accounting file pathname.

lf=*path*   Error-log file pathname.

lo=*filename*
           Lock filename.

lp=*device*   Device special file.

sd=*dir*   Spooling directory.

st=*filename*
           Status filename.

rm=*remote-host*
           Remote host.

rp=*remote-queue*
           Remote queue name.

rs[@]   Require remote users to have a local account.

LPRng /etc/printcap file

/etc/printcap relaxed syntax:

- All fields use an equals sign (=) to assign values (*name@* still turns off Boolean flags).
- Multiple line entries do not require a final backslash.
- No terminal colon is needed to designate field boundaries.

Additional attributes

lp=*queue@host*
           In addition to a local device, lp can be used to specify a remote printer and queue.

cm=*string*
           Descriptive (comment) string.

filter=*path*
           Specify the path for the external filter program.

server
           Entry applies only to jobs processed by the local lpd daemon.

force_localhost
> Force clients to use the local lpd daemon for spooling (rather than allowing lpr to do it).

oh=*list*
> Entry applies only on the listed hosts. The list can contain asterisks (wildcards); ! preceding a name serves as a negator.

bq=*queue*
> Designates the current entry as a bounce queue that will forward all jobs to the specified queue.

sv=*queue,queue…*
> Printer pool queue. Jobs will be divided among the listed queues. The component queues must include the ss=*queue* attribute, pointing to the pool queue.

destinations=*list*
router=*program-path*
> Send jobs to a destination in the list, based on the return value of the specified program.

tc=.*name*
> Include mechanism. Place the specified entry's attributes within this entry.

Variables available in printcap entries

%P Printer name.

%Q Queue name.

%h Simple hostname.

%H Fully qualified hostname.

%R Remote print queue name.

%M Remote computer hostname.

%D Current date.

LPRng lpd.perms file

ACCEPT|REJECT SERVICE=*code(s)* *KEYWORD(s)*

Specify access to printers, queues, daemons, and administrative commands. Accept or reject the requested operation if the conditions specified in the keywords are satisfied.

SERVICE codes include C (control jobs with lpc), R (spool jobs with lpr), M (remove jobs with lprm), Q (get status info with lpq), X (make connection to lpd), and P (general printing).

Keywords

USER | GROUP | HOST=*string(s)*
Match the user/group/host of applicable print jobs.

PRINTER=*string(s)*
Operation must be performed on a matching printer.

SERVER
Command must be executed on the local server.

REMOTEUSER | REMOTEGROUP | REMOTEHOST=*string(s)*
Match the user/group/host making the request (not always truly remote).

SAMEUSER *and* SAMEHOST
SAMEUSER requires USER to be the same as REMOTEUSER; SAMEHOST requires HOST to be the same as REMOTEHOST.

LPC=*subcommand-list*
Limit available lpc subcommands to those in the list.

DEFAULT *KEYWORD(s)*
Specify default matching criteria.

NOT
Reverse the logical sense of the comparison (i.e., to not matching).

The System V Spooling Subsystem

Used by HP-UX and Solaris.

---

lpstat   lpstat [*options*]

Display printer/queue status.

Options

-a*list*
Indicate whether the queues for the printers in *list* are accepting jobs.

-c*list*
> Display the members of the listed classes.

-o*list*
> List print requests (*list* may include request IDs, printer names, and class names, and all applicable jobs are displayed).

-p*list*
> Display the current status of the specified printers.

-u*list*
> Display the status of all jobs that belong to the specified users.

-v*list*
> Display the special file used by the specified printers.

-s Provide a summary; list all classes and their members and all printers and their associated devices.

-t Display all status information.

-d Display the system default destination.

---

cancel cancel *job(s)*|*printer(s)*

Cancel specific print jobs or the current job on the specified printer(s).

Options

-e Remove every job in the queue.

-I Limit the operation to local print jobs.

-u*user*
> Limit the operation to requests belonging to *user* (option may be used more than once).

---

lpmove lpmove *request-IDs*|*old-dest new_dest*

> Move the specified jobs (or all jobs in the *old-dest* queue) to the *new_dest* queue.

---

accept accept *printer(s)*
reject reject [-r"*reason*"] *printer(s)*

> Permit/inhibit jobs to be sent to the specified queue(s).

---

enable   enable *printer(s)*
disable   disable [-r"*reason*"] *printer(s)*

Start/stop printing on the specified printer(s).

---

lpshut   lpshut

Shutdown the spooling subsystem. You can restart it with the lp script in the *init.d* subdirectory (use the argument start).

---

lpadmin

lpadmin -p*printer* [*options*]
lpadmin -d*printer*

Administer printers and print queues, or set the system default destination (-d).

Options

-v*special-file* -e*printer*|-m*model-filename*|
  -i*program-path*

Add a printer. -e specifies the printer type by copying an existing printer's interface, -n specifies the printer by model type via the appropriate filename in */var/spool/lp/model*, and -i specifies the full path to a printer interface program.

-x*printer*

Remove the specified printer definition.

-c*class*

Place a printer into a class (can be combined with -v).

-r*class*

Remove a printer from a class.

-u*accesslist* (Solaris)

Specify users/hosts who can use this printer. Syntax:

    allow|deny:[*host*]\!*user*[,*user*...]

The *host* defaults to all hosts if it is omitted, and the user list can be replaced by the keyword all.

Remote printing

Remote queue options

HP-UX: `-orpqueue -ormhost`
Solaris: `-shost\!queue`

Daemon for incoming print requests

HP-UX: `rlpdaemon`   Solaris: `in.lpd`

Job priorities (HP-UX)

`lpadmin -Pprinter -gn`
> Set the default priority level for the specified printer to *n*.

`lpalt -pn job-ID`
> Modify the priority of the specified job.

`lpfence printer n`
> Set the specified printer's fence to *n* (minimum printing priority).

Job priorities (Solaris)

`lpusers -dn`
> Default priority level (the default is 20).

`lpusers -qn`
> Maximum priority a user can request (the default is 39).

`lpusers [-qn] user(s)`
> Set a user's priority limit to *n* (or back to the default limit).

`lp -ijob-ID -qn`
> Modify the specified job's priority.

`lp -jjob-ID -Himmediate`
> Move the specified job to the top of its queue. hold and resume can also be used with -H to suspend and resume a job.

lpalt (HP-UX)

`lpalt job-ID options`

Modify the specified print job.

Options

-n*n*   Change the number of copies to be printed to *n*.

-t*title*   Change the job title.

-d*queue*   Move the job to a new queue.

AIX Spooling Subsystem

AIX supports most BSD and System V administrative commands: lpq, lprm, lpstat, cancel, enable, disable, accept, and reject.

---

qmov   qmov -m *new-queue* [*options*]

Move jobs to a new queue.

Options

-# *n*
    Move job *n*.

-P *printer* [-u *user*]
    Move all jobs in the specified printer, or move all jobs belonging to the specified user.

---

qhld   qhld [-r] -# *m*|-P *printer*

Hold and release (-r) the specified print job or all jobs in the specified printer.

/etc/qconfig configuration file

```
queue-name:
  device = qdev1[,qdev2 …]
  attribute = value
  …
qdev1:
  backend = /usr/lpd/piobe
  attribute = value
  …
[qdev2:
  …]
```

Define queue and queue devices.

Queue attributes

`acctfile = path`
Accounting file pathname.

`device = devname[, devname …]`
List of associated device names.

`discipline = fcfs|sjn`
Job selection algorithm: first come, first served (default), or shortest job next.

`up = TRUE|FALSE`
Whether the queue is enabled.

Device attributes

`access = write|both`
Available access to printer device: either write or read/write (the default).

`align = TRUE|FALSE`
Whether to send a form feed before starting a job if the printer is idle.

`backend = path`
Path to the backend program.

`file = device`
Special file associated with the device (as defined in the ODM).

`header|trailer = never|always|group`
When a header/trailer page should be placed before a job (group means "print only once for multi-file print jobs").

Remote printing

Queue definition syntax

```
queue:
    rq = remote-queue
    host = remote-host
    backend = /usr/lib/lpd/rembak
```

`startsrc -s lpd`
Start the daemon for incoming LPD print requests.

Serial Lines

Termcap/terminfo file

AIX:	*/usr/lib/terminfo*
FreeBSD:	*/etc/termcap* (a link to */usr/share/misc/termcap*)
Linux:	*/etc/termcap* and */usr/share/terminfo*
HP-UX:	*/usr/lib/terminfo* (a link to */usr/share/lib/terminfo*)
Solaris:	*/etc/termcap* and */usr/share/lib/terminfo*

stty   stty *options* [*value*] …

Modify serial line settings.

Options

n	Baud rate.
rows *n*	Lines on the screen.
columns *n*	Columns on the screen.
[-]echo	Echo/don't echo typed characters on the screen.
erase *c*	Delete the previous character.
kill *c*	Erase the entire command line.
intr *c*	Interrupt the foreground command.
eof *c*	End-of-file signal.
susp *c*	Suspend the foreground command.
lnext *c*	Interpret the next character literally (used to insert control characters into the command line).
werase *c*	Erase the previous word.
rprnt *c*	Reprint the pending command line.
stop *c*	Pause terminal input and output.
start *c*	Restart a paused terminal.
flush *c*	Discard all pending (undisplayed) output.

quit *c*	Kill the foreground command and dump core.
oddp	Enable odd parity.
evenp	Enable even parity.
-parity	No parity is generated or detected.
cstopb	Use two stop bits (-cstopb means one stop bit).
clocal	Use a hard carrier (-clocal means soft).
sane	Reset many options to reasonable settings.

Serial Line Configuration Files

/etc/ttys (FreeBSD)

port command type [*flags*]

port	Special file in */dev* that communicates with this serial line.
"*command*"	getty command init should run for this serial line.
type	Terminal type (from */etc/termcap*), the network keyword (for pseudo terminals), or dialin (for dial-up modems).
flags	Keywords, separated by spaces:

	on|off	*Is line enabled?*
	secure	*Allow root logins.*
	window=cmd	*init should run cmd before the command in field 2.*
	group=name	*Define group of teminals for /etc/login.conf.*

/etc/inittab (AIX, HP-UX, Linux, Solaris)

Terminal-related entries have a getty command as their final field (see page 31 for more about the inittab file).

getty programs

Usual:	*/usr/sbin/getty*	FreeBSD:	*/usr/libexec/getty*
Linux:	*/sbin/mgetty*		
	/sbin/mingetty (for the console)		

Networking

ifconfig
```
ifconfig lo0 localhost up
ifconfig interface ip-address netmask mask
```

The first form configures the loopback interface. The second form assigns the specified IPv4 address and subnet mask to *interface*. FreeBSD and Solaris allow you to replace the address and netmask parameters (including the keywords) with a CIDR address.

Displaying information about network interfaces

```
ifconfig [options] [interface]
```

Display the configuration of the specified interface(s).

-a Display data for all interfaces (not supported by HP-UX).

-l *(FreeBSD and AIX)*
    List all network interfaces.

Network interface configuration files

AIX: Stored in the ODM; modify with mktcpip or SMIT.

FreeBSD: */etc/rc.conf*:

```
hostname="name"
ifconfig_iface="ip-addr netmask mask"
```

HP-UX: */etc/rc.config.d/netconf*:

```
HOSTNAME="name"
INTERFACE_NAME[n]=name
IP_ADDRESS[n]=addr
SUBNET_MASK[n]=mask
INTERFACE_STATE[n]=up|down
```

n is the interface number (starting at 0).

Linux: /etc/sysconfig/networking/devices/ifcfg-ethn Red Hat
         /etc/sysconfig/network/ifcfg-eth n   SuSE

         DEVICE=*name*   Red Hat
         BOOTPROTO=static|dhcp
         IPADDR=*addr*
         NETMASK=*mask*
         ONBOOT=yes|no   Red Hat only
         STARTMODE=yes|no   SuSE only

         /etc/sysconfig/network: Red Hat

         HOSTNAME="*name*"

         /etc/HOSTNAME:
         Holds the hostname (SuSE).

Solaris: /etc/hostname.iface:
         The first line holds the hostname. Any additional
         line(s) hold ifconfig command arguments
         (optional).

Displaying the system's MAC address

AIX: entstat *adapter*   HP-UX: lanscan
FreeBSD, Linux, Solaris: ifconfig *interface*

CIDR suffixes and subnet masks

Suffix	Subnet mask	Max. hosts
/22	255.255.252.0	1022
/23	255.255.254.0	510
/24	255.255.255.0	254
/25	255.255.255.128	126
/26	255.255.255.192	62
/27	255.255.255.224	30
/28	255.255.255.240	14
/29	255.255.255.248	6
/30	255.255.255.252	2

Important services and their associated ports

Unless otherwise noted, services are assigned to both the TCP and UPD ports; port numbers followed by an "s" are used by the secure version of the service.

Service	Ports	Service	Ports
DHCP client	68	DHCP server	67
DNS	53	Finger	79
Ftp	20,21,990s,998s	HTTP	80,443s
IMAP 2	143	Kerberos	88,749-50
IMAP 3	220	LDAP	389,636s
IMAP 4	993s	LPD	515
NetBIOS	137-139	NFS	2049
NTP	123	NFS (Solaris)	4045/udp
POP-2	109	Rexec	512/tcp
POP-3	110,995s	Rlogin	513/tcp
Routed	520	RPC	111
Rsh	514/tcp	Rsync	873
SSH	22	SMB	445
SMTP	25,465s	SNMP	161
Syslog	514/udp	SNMP traps	162
reliable Syslog	601	Telnet	23,992s
TFtp	69	X11	6000-19,6063
		X11 font server	7100

Network Client Configuration

Name service configuration

/etc/hosts file

ip-addr   *hostname* [*hostname* ...]

Each entry associates an IP address with one or more hostnames.

DNS client configuration: /etc/resolv.conf

Configures the resolver (DNS client). *letc/resolv.conf* generally begins with a *search* directive, followed by an ordered list of *nameserver* entries.

search *domain*
> Search this domain for names.

nameserver *ip-address*
> Specify a name server to contact for name resolution. When necessary, name servers are contacted in the order listed. There may be a maximum of 3 nameserver entries.

sortlist *network-list*
> Select among multiple name resolution responses by choosing subnets in the order specified.

options ndots:*n*
> Add domain names to all names that contain fewer than *n* periods.

Name service switch file: /etc/nsswitch.conf

item: *source* [*source* [*source* ...]]

Specifies the ordering among multiple services. Used by HP-UX, Linux, and Solaris (will also be used by FreeBSD 5).

Item is the set of information, generally named for a traditional configuration file in */etc*: e.g., hosts (name resolution), passwd (user account data), etc.

The remainder of each entry is an ordered list of one or more information sources: files (usual configuration file), dns (DNS name service), nis (NIS service), ldap (LDAP service), etc.

FreeBSD: /etc/host.conf

This file is similar to the name service switch file. It orders the available name services, one keyword per line, and uses bind instead of dns.

AIX: /etc/netsvc.conf

item = *source*[, *source*]

This file is similar in purpose to the name service switch file, although the syntax is slightly different. The keywords local and bind are used instead of hosts and dns.

---

route route *op* [-net] *dest* [netmask *mask*] *gateway*

Modify the static routing table. *op* is a keyword that indicates the operation to perform: e.g., add (add a new entry) or delete (remove an entry). add can be optionally followed by default to set the default route.

AIX, FreeBSD, and Solaris also support change (modify an entry) and flush (remove all entries); HP-UX provides the latter functionality via the -f option.

dest is the destination host or network, *mask* is the netmask, and *gateway* is the gateway used to reach the specified destination.

Static routing configuration files

AIX: Routes created with the route command are stored in the ODM automatically.

FreeBSD: */etc/rc.conf*:

```
defaultrouter="ip-addr"
static_routes="name [name …]"
route_name="route add args"
```

HP-UX: */etc/rc.config.d/netconf*:

```
ROUTE_DESTINATION[n]=ip-addr|default
ROUTE_MASK[n]="mask"
ROUTE_GATEWAY[n]="ip-addr"
ROUTE_ARGS[n]="additional-route-args"
```

n is the interface number (starting at 0).

Red Hat: */etc/sysconfig/network* defines the default gateway.

```
GATEWAY="ip-addr"
```

/etc/sysconfig/static-routes defines static routes.

```
interface host|net destination gateway
ip-addr
```

SuSE: */etc/sysconfig/network/routes* defines static routes (including the default).

```
destination gateway netmask device
```

Solaris: */etc/defaultrouter* holds IP address(es) for default router(s).

DHCP client configuration

Enabling DHCP

AIX: Use smit mktcpip.

FreeBSD: /etc/rc.conf:

    ifconfig_iface="DHCP"

HP-UX: /etc/rc.config.d/netconf:

    IFCONFIG_n="dhcpclient"

Linux: /etc/sysconfig/network-scripts/ifcfg-ethn:

    BOOTPROTO="dhcp"   Red Hat; SuSE 8 stores the file
                             in /etc/sysconfig/network.

Solaris: Existence of the file /etc/dhcp.iface (iface is the interface
           name).

DHCP configuration files

AIX: /etc/dhcpcd.ini   FreeBSD: /etc/dhclient.conf
Solaris: /etc/default/dhcpagent

DHCP client command/daemon

AIX: dhcpcd daemon   FreeBSD: dhclient command
HP-UX: dhcpclient daemon   Linux: dhcpcd daemon
Solaris: dhcpagent daemon

Current lease information

AIX: /usr/tmp/dhcpcd.log FreeBSD: /var/db/dhclient.leases
HP-UX: /etc/auto_parms.log Solaris: /etc/dhcp/iface.dhc
Linux: /var/lib/dhcpcd/dhcpcd-ethn-info (SuSE)

Network Servers

inetd

TCP/IP super daemon, manages many subordinate daemons,
starting them as needed.

Configuration file: /etc/inetd.conf

```
[#]service socket protocol wait|nowait user program args
```

The fields hold the service name (as defined in */etc/services*), the socket type, the protocol, whether to wait for the command to return when it is started, the user who should run the command, and the command to run, along with its arguments. An initial # deactivates (comments out) the entry.

TCP wrappers[†]

Provide finer access control and enhanced logging for inetd-based services. Configuration file entries are modified so that the tcpd daemon precedes the program name:

```
/usr/sbin/tcpd original-program
```

Access control is provided by the */etc/hosts.allow* and */etc/hosts.deny* configuration files. Entry syntax is as follows:

```
service : hosts-domains-subnets
```

Allows/denies access to the specified service from the listed remote locations. The list can include the LOCAL (localhost) and EXCEPT keywords (inverts allow/deny sense).

The recommended final line in */etc/hosts.deny* is:

```
ALL : ALL :
```

xinetd (Linux)

This package has different configuration file formats. It also includes some TCP Wrappers features within the daemon itself.

Configuration files

/etc/xinetd
  Sets default values for all services. Syntax:

```
defaults
{
attribute = value
...
}
includedir /etc/xinetd.d          Service-specific files go here.
```

/etc/xinetd.d/*

    Per-service configuration files. Syntax:

```
service name
{
attribute = value
…
}
```

Attributes for traditional inetd fields

```
socket_type = type
protocol = proto
wait = yes|no
user = user
server = /path
server-args = args
```

Other attributes

```
log_type = SYSLOG facility
```
    Log events to the specified syslog facility (e.g., authpriv).

```
log_on_success = items (also log_on_failure)
```
    Include this data in log messages. Items include HOST, PID, and USERID. In service stanzas, use += to add to the default list for a specific service.

```
instances = n
```
    Maximum running daemon processes (per server).

```
disable = yes|no
```
    Determine whether service is enabled or not.

```
only_from = hosts
no_access = hosts
```
    Limit/deny access to the listed hosts.

```
access_times = hh:mm-hh:mm
```
    Allowed access times (using a 24-hour clock).

DNS

named.conf location (main configuration file)

Usual: */etc*   FreeBSD: */etc/namedb*

Default hints filename

FreeBSD: *named.root*   Linux: *root.hint*

Boot script configuration file

FreeBSD: */etc/rc.conf*: enable="YES", named_flags="*args*"
Linux: */etc/sysconfig/named*: ROOTDIR=*chroot-dir*,
           OPTIONS="*named-args*"

Main configuration file: named.conf

options

    Set global options (all are optional).

```
options {
  allow-query { list; };          Accept queries only
                                  from the specified servers.
  allow-transfer { list; };       Limit zone transfers
                                  to the specified servers.
  allow-notify { list; };  Sources for update notifications.
  also-notify { list; };   Additional update notice list.
  blackhole { list; };     Completely ignore these hosts.
  directory "path";        Default directory for relative
                           pathnames.
  forward only|first;      Use forwarding exclusively/first.
  forwarders { list; };    Forward external queries to list.
  maintain-ixfr-base yes|no;      BIND 8; save data for
                                  incremental transfers.
  notify yes|no|explicit;  BIND 9; update notices?
                           (explicit = list only).
  provide-ixfr yes|no;     BIND 9; use incremental zone
                           transfers.
  pid-file "path";         File holding named process's PID.
  request-xfer yes|no;     Request incremental zone transfers.
};
```

zone

    Define a zone and its attributes (only type is required).

```
zone "name" {
  type keyword;        Server type: master, slave, forward, etc.
  file "path";         Pathname to zone file.
  masters { list; }; List of master name servers.
  allow-query { list; };       Accept queries only
                               from these servers.
  allow-transfer { list; };    Send zone transfers only
                               to list.
  allow-update { list; }; Valid sources for dynamic updates.
```

```
            allow-update-forwarding { list; };
                            BIND 9; sources for forwardable updates.
            also-notify { list; };
                            Send update notices to all slaves plus these.
            forward only|first;     Use forwarding exclusively/first.
            forwarders { list; };   Forward external queries here.
            notify yes|no|explicit;
                            BIND 9; update notices? (explicit = list only).
            update-policy { rule-list; };
                            BIND 9; who can update what; Rules syntax:
                            grant|deny who-key what where [types]
        };
```

logging

Specify logging behavior.

```
        logging {
          channel name {              Define log target.
              syslog facility;        Send messages to this facility.
              [severity level;]       Specify syslog severity level.
            | file "path";            Send messages to this file.
            | null;                   Discard messages.
          };
          [channel …]
          [category keywords { channel-list; };]
                            Link message types to channel(s).
          [category default { channel-list; };]
                            Default channel(s).
        };
```

Useful channels include general, config (configuration file
processing), network[BIND 9] (network operations), notify (update
notifications), queries, security (request approvals/denials),
update (dynamic updates), and xfer-in and xfer-out (zone trans-
fers received/sent).

server

Define how to communicate with a specific name server.

```
        server ip-address {
          [provide-ixfr yes|no;]   BIND 9; provide IXFR
                                   to this server.
          [request-ixfr yes|no;]   BIND 9; request IXFR
                                   from this server.
          [support-ixfr yes|no;]   BIND 8; server supports
                                   incremental zone transfers.
          [keys { key; };]         TSIG key to use with this server.
        };
```

acl

Define an IP address match list.

```
acl "name" {
  [!] match-string; …
};
```

Each match string can be an IP or network address or the name of another address list. ! = do not match.

key

Define a key (shared secret security).

```
key "name" {
  algorithm hmac-md5;    This is the only supported algorithm.
  secret "encoded-key";
};
```

Encode the key using dnskeygen[BIND 8] or dnssec-keygen[BIND 9]..

view

Define a BIND 9 view.

```
view "name" {
  match-clients { list; };        Hosts that access
                                  zone through view.
  zone "zone-name" { … }; Zone(s) as defined in this view.
  [zone …]                Other options for this view.
  [other-options]
};
```

controls

Specifies ndc/rndc server access. Allow listed hosts to manage this name server with rndc via the specified address, using cryptographic keys.

```
controls {                        BIND 9 version
  inet addr allow { hosts; } keys { keys; };
};
```

include

Inserts the contents of an external file.

```
include "path";
```

Zone file records

entity-name [*ttl*] IN *keyword data*

entity is the item being defined, *ttl* is an optional time-to-live value (cache lifetime in seconds), *keyword* indicates the record type, and *data* is definition data for this entity.

SOA
   Start of authority record (basic zone parameters).

   ```
   @ IN SOA hostname admin (
       s    ;   Serial number (32-bit).
       time ;   Slave update check interval.
       time ;   Failed update retry interval.
       time ;   Discard timeout if master is down.
       time ;   TTL for negative replies[BIND 9]/cached data[BIND 8].
   )
   ```

   time syntax is: *n*[s|m|h|d|w] (the code letter indicates units).

zone IN NS server-hostname
   Name server definition.

hostname IN A IP-address
   Hostname-to-IP address mapping.

alias IN CNAME hostname
   Host alias definition.

hostname IN MX priority mail-server
   Designate a mail server for a host. *priority* is an integer (lower
   numbers indicate more favored servers).

host-part-of-IP-address IN PTR hostname
   IP address-to-hostname mapping.

_service._proto.domain IN SRV priority weight port host
   SRV: advertise an available service.

hostname IN AAAA IPv6-address
   AAAA: IPv6 hostname-to-address mapping.

Zone file directives

$TTL seconds
   Default TTL for cached address mappings.

$ORIGIN domain
   Specify/change the default domain context.

$GENERATE range record-template
   Generate resource records automatically.

$INCLUDE path
   Insert an external file's contents.

---

ndc (BIND 8) and rndc (BIND 9)

Manipulate the name server process. Both utilities have the following subcommands:

stop

    Terminate the server process after any pending updates are complete.

halt

    Stop the server immediately.

reload [*zone*]

    Cause the server to reload its configuration and all specified zone file(s).

dumpdb *and* stats

    Write the cache contents and server statistics to a log file (by default, *named_dump.db* and *named.stats*, respectively).

restart[BIND 8]

    Restart the server.

Determining the BIND version

dig @*host* version.bind txt chaos

Direct named to display its version string. The information will be accurate only if this string has not been modified by the network administrator.

DHCP server

Open source operating systems typically use the DHCP server provided by the Internet Software Consortium (ISC).

Server location

ISC:	*/usr/sbin/dhcpd*	AIX:	*/usr/sbin/dhcpsd*
HP-UX:	*/usr/lbin/bootpd*		
Solaris:	*/usr/lib/inet/in.dhcpd*		

Configuration file

ISC:	*/etc/dhcpd.conf*	AIX:	*/etc/dhcpsd.cnf*
HP-UX:	*/etc/dhcptab*		
Solaris:	*/var/dhcp/dhcptab* and network files in */var/dhcp*		

Boot script configuration file

Red Hat: */etc/sysconfig/dhcpd*:

    DHCPDARGS="*args*"

SuSE: */etc/sysconfig/dhcpd*:

    DHCP_INTERFACE="eth*n*"
    DHCP_RUN_CHROOTED
    DHCP_RUN_AS="*user*"
    DHCP_OTHER_ARGS="*args*"

Solaris*:   */etc/inet/dhcpsvc.conf*:

    DAEMON_ENABLED="TRUE"

Leases data files

ISC: */var/lib/dhcp/dhcpd.leases*
AIX: */etc/dhcpsd.ar*, */etc/dhcpsd.cr*
HP-UX: */var/tmp/bootp.dump*
Solaris: network files in */var/dhcp*

DHCP relay server

Open source operating systems typically use the DHCP relay
server provided by the Internet Software Consortium (ISC).

Server location

ISC: */usr/sbin/dhcrelay*   AIX: */usr/sbin/dhcprd*
Solaris: */usr/lib/inet/in.dhcpd*

Configuration file

AIX: */etc/dhcprd.cnf*

Boot script configuration file

SuSE: */etc/sysconfig/dhcpd*:

    DHCRELAY_INTERFACES="eth*n*"
    DHCRELAY_SERVERS="*host*"

Solaris: */etc/inet/dhcpsvc.conf*:

    DAEMON_ENABLED=TRUE
    RUN_MODE=*relay*
    RELAY_DESTINATIONS=*server*

---

* Solaris 8 uses the file */etc/default/dhcp*.

SNMP server

Open source operating systems typically use the Net-SNMP server.

Primary agent daemon

AIX:	*/usr/sbin/snmpd*	HP-UX:	*/usr/sbin/snmpdm*
Net-SNMP:	*/usr/local/sbin/snmpd*		
	/usr/sbin/snmpd under SuSE Linux		
Solaris:	*/usr/lib/snmp/snmpdx*		

Agent configuration file(s)

AIX: */etc/snmpd.conf*
HP-UX: */etc/SnmpAgent.d/snmpd.conf*
Net-SNMP: */usr/local/share/snmp/snmpd.conf*
           /usr/share/snmp/snmpd.conf under SuSE Linux
Solaris: */etc/snmp/conf/snmpdx.** and
        /etc/snmp/conf/snmpd.conf

MIB files

AIX: */etc/mib.defs*
HP-UX: */etc/SnmpAgent.d/snmpinfo.dat*
        */opt/OV/snmp_mibs/** (OpenView)
Net-SNMP: */usr/share/snmp/mibs/**
Solaris: */var/snmp/mib/**

snmptranslate

        snmptranslate [*options*] *item*

        Display information about MIB entries.

Useful options

snmptranslate -Tp .*oid**
    Display MIB subtree.

snmptranslate -Td .*oid*
    Text description for OID.

---

* Remember that absolute OIDs begin with a period.

```
snmptranslate -IR -On name
    Show full OID name (mib-2 subtree only).

snmptranslate -IR name
    Translate OID name to number.

snmptranslate -On .numeric-oid
    Translate numeric OID to name.

snmptranslate -Td `snmptranslate -IR -On leaf`
    Display full OID string and numeric equivalent for
    leaf.
```

Networking Administrative Commands

arp   `arp -a [-n]`

Display address resolution protocol (ARP) tables. The -n
option says to display the numeric host address (useful
when DNS is unavailable/suspect).

hostname

`hostname [name]`

Display or set the hostname.

nfsstat   `nfsstat [options]`

Display NFS statistics.

Options

-rc Display client statistics.

-s   Display server statistics.

-n   Exclude RPC statistics.

nslookup

`nslookup [options] [host] [name-server]`

Query Internet name servers. Without arguments, the
command starts an interactive session.

Subcommands

item

> Retrieve records for this item (interpreted as a host-name by default).

set type=*record-type*

> Type of records to return (the default is A).

server *host*

> Use this server for queries.

exit

> End session.

---

netstat netstat [*options*] [*rsecs*]

Without arguments, lists all active network connections with the local host.

If the argument is included, the display is continuous and is refreshed every *rsecs* seconds. On Linux systems, the -c option is used instead (refresh interval = 1 second).

Options

-a   Include passive connections in the connections list.

-r   Display routing tables.

-i   Display a summary of the network interfaces.

-I *interface*

> Limit the display to the specified network interface. On Linux systems, the *interface* parameter is used with -i.

-s   Display statistics for each network protocol.

-p *proto*

> Limit the display to the specified protocol. On Linux systems, use the --raw, --upd, or --tcp option instead.

-n   Display network addresses as numbers (useful when DNS is unavailable or suspect).

ping   ping *host* [*packet-size count*]   *AIX, HP-UX*
            ping -c *count* [-s *packet-size*] *host* *AIX, FreeBSD, Linux*
            ping -s *host packet-size count*   *Solaris*

Check network connectivity with a remote host. The second and third forms listed ping the specified host *count* times and then display summary statistics. *packet-size* is the desired packet size. When only a hostname is specified, the command will ping continuously until interrupted (except under Solaris, which pings only once).

---

traceroute

     traceroute [-n] *destination*

Display the route to a remote destination. The -n option says to display a numeric host address (useful when DNS is unavailable/suspect).

Electronic Mail

/etc/aliases file

alias: *name* [*name* ...]

Define a mail alias as the specified list of user(s) and/or other aliases. Aliases can be nested. An initial backslash defines a terminal alias (not subject to further expansion).

This file is stored in */etc/mail/aliases* under FreeBSD and HP-UX.

sendmail

File/directory locations

Boot script configuration file

FreeBSD: */etc/rc.conf*:

          sendmail_enable="YES"

HP-UX: */etc/rc.config.d/mailservs*:

          export SENDMAIL_SERVER=1

Linux: /etc/sysconfig/sendmail:
           START_SENDMAIL="yes"
Solaris: /etc/default/sendmail:
           DAEMON=yes

sendmail.cf directory

Usual: /etc/mail
AIX: /etc   Linux: /etc

Configuration file build area

AIX: /usr/samples/tcpip/sendmail/cf
FreeBSD: /usr/share/sendmail/cf/cf
HP-UX: /usr/newconfig/etc/mail/cf/cf
Linux: /usr/share/sendmail-cf/cf (Red Hat)
          /usr/share/sendmail/cf (SuSE)
Solaris: /usr/lib/mail/cf

syslog mail facility messages

FreeBSD: /var/log/maillog
HP-UX: /var/adm/syslog/mail.log
Linux: /var/log/maillog (Red Hat), /var/log/mail (SuSE)
Solaris: /var/adm/messages

---

sendmail

sendmail [options]

Main sendmail server program.

Options

-bd -qnm
   Run as a daemon, checking the queue every n
   minutes.

-bp
   List the sendmail work queue (/var/queue/mqueue).

-bt
   Interactive address translation mode. Subcommands:

   /mx host   List MX records for host.
   /map map-name address   Translate a mapped address.

/try smtp *address*	Address translation for mailer/ recipient. Use /tryflags S for /try to apply to senders.

-bv *address*
> Validate the specified address.

-oQ*path* **-q**
> Process the specified queue immediately.

-d*level.sublevel*
> Debug mode (output goes to syslog). Useful levels:
>
> | -d0 | Show version, compile flags, and host/ domain. |
> |---|---|
> | -d0.15 | Also display defined mailers, with flags ("F="). |
> | -d8.7 | Show DNS name resolution process. |
> | -d11.2 | Trace the delivery process. |
> | -d17 | Show MX hosts. |
> | -d27 | Show alias translation. |
> | -d34.11 | Trace header generation. |
> | -d35.9 | Display internal macro values (e.g., $k). |
> | -d37 | Display options as they are set. |
> | -d37.8 | Also show each item added to class lists. |
> | -d40 | Watch queue processing. |
> | -d60 | Display map lookup operations. |

Building the sendmail.cf configuration file

```
cd build-dir
edit name.mc
./Build name.cf
cp /etc/mail/sendmail.cf /etc/mail/sendmail.cf.save
cp name.cf /etc/mail/sendmail.cf|
chmod 444 /etc/mail/sendmail.cf
kill -HUP `head -1 /var/run/sendmail.pid`
```

Configuration source file macros

Note the unusual quoting style: `` `item' ``

Defined macros

```
define(`ALIAS_FILE',`path')
```
Location of aliases file.

```
undefine(`ALIAS_FILE')
```
Disable aliases file.

```
define(`confCON_EXPENSIVE',`True')
```
Hold (don't transport) mail for expensive mailers.

```
define(`confDEF_USER_ID',`user:group')
```
Default server user and group.

```
define(`confEBINDIR',`path')
```
Location of smrsh and mail.local.

```
define(`confFALLBACK_MX',`host')
```
Send bounced/bogus mail here.

```
define(`confFORWARD_FILE',`path[:path…]')
```
Path to search for forward files ($z = ~).

```
define(`confLDAP_DEFAULT_SPEC', `-h host -b root-key')
```
Specify the LDAP server and root key.

```
define(`confMAX_DAEMON_CHILDREN',n)
```
Maximum child processes.

```
define(`confMAX_MESSAGE_SIZE',bytes)
```
Largest acceptable message.

```
define(`confMIN_FREE_BLOCKS',blocks)
```
Required filesystem free space.

```
define(`confMIN_QUEUE_AGE',`time')
```
Messages stay in queue for at least as long as *time*.

```
define(`confPRIVACY_FLAGS',`flag-list')
```
SMTP privacy options.

```
define(`confQUEUE_LA',lavg)
```
Queue all incoming mail when load average is above *lavg*.

```
define(`confREFUSE_LA',lavg)
```
Refuse connections when the load average is above *lavg*.

```
define(`confSAFE_FILE_ENV',`path')
```
Pipe mail only to regular files under the specified path.

```
define(`confSERVICE_SWITCH_FILE',`path')
```
Location of network services switch file (when not provided
by the operating system).

```
define(`confTO_parameter',n)
```
Set the timeout length.

```
define(`CONNECTION_RATE_THROTTLE',n)
```
Accept only *n* connections per second.

```
define(`LOCAL_MAILER_PATH',`path')
define(`LOCAL_MAILER_ARGS',`command')
```
Path to/command for the local mailer program executable.

```
define(`LOCAL_RELAY',`host')
FEATURE(`stickyhost')
```
Send mail addressed to unqualified names to *host*. Sticky host
says to do so even if the MAIL_HUB feature is also used.

```
define(`LOCAL_SHELL_PATH',`path')
define(`LOCAL_SHELL_ARGS',`command')
```
Path to/command for shell program for piped messages.

```
define(`MAIL_HUB',`host')
```
Send local mail to a different host.

```
define(`mailer_MAILER_PATH',`path')
define(`mailer_MAILER_ARGS',`command')
```
Path to/command for the specified mailer's program.

```
define(`mailer_MAILER_FLAGS',`addl-flags')
```
Add flags to the usual set for the specified mailer.

```
define(`mailer_MAILER_MAX',bytes)
```
Maximum message size for the specified mailer.

```
define(`mailer_RELAY',`host')
```
Relay mail for the specified mailer.

```
define(`PROCMAIL_MAILER_PATH',`path')
```
Path to procmail.

```
define(`SMART_HOST',`host')
```
Send all nonlocal mail to this host.

```
define(`SMTP_MAILER_FLAGS',`e')
```
Make the SMTP mailer "expensive."

```
define(`STATUS_FILE',`path')
```
Location of statistics file.

Standalone macros

```
DOMAIN(`name')
```
Include the *../domain/*name.*m4* file.

```
EXPOSED_USER(`user')
```
Exclude *user* from masquerading.

```
FEATURE(`access_db', `dbtype  path')
```
Use the specified access database.

```
FEATURE(`allmasquerade')
```
Masquerade recipients too.

```
FEATURE(`always_add_domain')
```
Add domain to unqualified names.

```
FEATURE(`blacklist_recipients')
```
Allow incoming address entries in the access map.

```
FEATURE(`delay_checks'[, `friend'])
```
Reverse the order of access checks. If the argument is included, enable the SPAMFRIEND feature (overrides checks).

```
FEATURE(`dnsbl'[,`server'])
```
Use the Internet blacklist on the specified server.

```
FEATURE(`generics_entire_domain')
```
Use the generics table for hosts in subdomains of any relevant domain.

```
FEATURE(`genericstable',`dbtype  path')
```
Use the specified generics table map for rewriting outgoing sender addresses.

```
FEATURE(`ldap_routing')
```
Use LDAP for mail routing.

```
FEATURE(`local_lmtp'[,`path-to-mail.local'])
```
Use mail.local as the local mailer for pipes to files and programs (optionally, giving the path to the executable).

```
FEATURE(`local_procmail')
```
Use procmail as the local mailer.

FEATURE(`masquerade_envelope')
     Masquerade envelope as well as headers.

FEATURE(`msp')
     Use separate MTA and MSA processes.

FEATURE(`nocanonify')
     Defer DNS lookups (usually to the mail hub).

FEATURE(`nullclient',`mailhub')
     Send all mail to the specified server for processing.

FEATURE(`redirect')
     Enable .REDIRECT alias suffix support for users who have left
     the organization.

FEATURE(`relay_entire_domain')
     Perform relaying for any host in a local domain.

FEATURE(`smrsh'[,`path-to-smrsh'])
     Use smrsh for piped email messages (path is optional).

FEATURE(`use_cw_file')
define(`confCW_FILE',`path')
     Define local hosts and domains in a file; specify its path.

FEATURE(`virtuser_entire_domain')
     Use the virtual user table for hosts in subdomains of any rele-
     vant domain.

FEATURE(`virtusertable',`dbtype path')
     Use the specified virtual user table map for routing incoming
     addresses.

GENERICS_DOMAIN(`domain')
GENERICS_DOMAIN_FILE(`path')
     Use the generics table for the specified domain or domains
     listed in the specified file.

LDAP_ROUTE_DOMAIN(`ldap-domain')
LDAP_ROUTE_DOMAIN_FILE(`path')
     Use LDAP routing for the specified domain or the domains
     listed in the specified file.

LOCAL_USER(`name')
     Exclude a specified user from the effect of LOCAL_RELAY.

LUSER_RELAY(`host, address-or-error')
    Destination/error for invalid local addresses.

MASQUERADE_AS(`domain')
    Make all messages appear to be coming from the specified
    domain.

MASQUERADE_EXCEPTION(`host|domain')
    Don't apply masquerading to this host/domain.

MODIFY_MAILER_FLAGS(`mailer',`+|-flags')
    Add/remove the specified flags from the default list for the
    indicated mailer.

OSTYPE(`name')
    Specify an operating system.

RELAY_DOMAIN(`domain')
RELAY_DOMAIN_FILE(`path')
    Relay messages for the specified domain or the domains listed
    in the specified file.

VERSIONID(`string')
    Identify the version of the configuration source file.

VIRTUSER_DOMAIN(`domain')
VIRTUSER_DOMAIN_FILE(`path')
    Use the virtual user table for the specified domain or the
    domains listed in the specified file.

procmail and fetchmail

Invoking procmail

procmail can be used for mail filtering when it is the mail delivery
agent. Individual users can also use it via a *.forward* file, such as
the following (in *$HOME*):

```
"|IFS=' ' && exec /usr/bin/procmail -Yf- || exit 75 #user"
```

/etc/procmailrc and $HOME/.procmailrc configuration files

HOME=/path
    Root for relative pathnames. You can also set the usual SHELL
    and PATH environment variables.

`ORGMAIL=`*path*
> Location of the incoming mail file.

`MAILDIR=`*path*
> root directory for the mail message tree.

`DEFAULT=`*path*
> Default mail message destination file.

`LOGFILE=`*path*
> Log file location.

Recipe syntax

`:0[`*flags*`][:[`*lock-file*`]]`	*Indicates the start of a new recipe.*
`* condition`	*Zero or more lines of regular expressions.*
`disposition`	*Destination/treatment of matching messages.*

For each recipe, each successive message is compared to the specified regular expression(s), and the disposition is applied if it matches. Otherwise, the message moves on to the next recipe in the configuration file.

The final colon in the initial lines specifies that a lock file be used (using the specified path, if included).

Multiple asterisk lines must all match (AND logic). To create an OR condition, use parentheses and the regular expression | character.

Dispositions

file
> Send to mail (can be */dev/null*).

`!`*user*
> Send mail to *user*.

`|`*command*
> Pipe message to *command* (often `formail`—see the section on this command).

Flags

Flags specify which part of the message is searched for the regular expressions. The defaults are `Hbh` (i.e., the body is not searched).

H   Search the message headers.

B   Search the message body.

---

h   Apply disposition the message header.

b   Apply disposition to the message body.

c   Perform the operation on a copy of the message.

D   Perform case-sensitive regular expression matching.

f   Recipe is a filter only; matching messages remain in the input stream.

A   Chain this recipe to the immediately preceding one, executing only when a message has matched the patterns in the preceding recipe (which will have included the f flag).

E   Process this recipe only when the preceding recipe's conditions did not match the current message (i.e., create an ELSE condition).

w   Wait for the filter program to complete, and check its exit code before continuing on to the next recipe. The W form does the same thing while suppressing any "Program failure" messages.

---

formail   formail [options]

Formats a mail message on standard input according to the options, placing the new message on standard output (where it can be appended to a file, piped to sendmail -t -oi, etc.).

Options

-r   Generate a reply, deleting existing headers and body.

-X|-x header
       Retain/just extract the named message header (can be used more than once).

-k   Keep the message body when using -r or -x.

-a header:text
       Append the specified header if it is not already present (-A appends unconditionally).

-I *header*:*text*
> Replace the existing header line (-i renames the current one).

-z Clean up header formatting.

---

fetchmail

fetchmail [options] [host]

Retrieve mail according to the command arguments and/or configuration file.

Options

-d *seconds*
> Run in daemon mode with the specified polling interval. Terminate with fetchmail -quit.

-f *path*
> Specify the configuration file location (defaults to *$HOME/.fetchmailrc*).

Configuration file entries

set daemon *seconds*
> Set the polling interval when fetchmail is run as a daemon.

set logfile *path*
> Enable logging to the specified file.

set [no]syslog
> Use/don't use syslog for messages (fetchmail logs to the mail facility, using the info, alert, and err severity levels).

defaults *settings*
> Specify defaults for various settings.

poll host [via *vhost*]
> Define a remote mail server. When the via attribute is included, *host* functions as a target name for the fetchmail command only, and *vhost* is the system actually contacted.

[proto *protocol*]
> Connection protocol to use (e.g., pop3, imap, or etrn).

[user *remote-user* [is *local-user* here]
[password *string*] [auth *type*]
> Specifies the user account on the remote server (optionally, mapping to a local account). *string* is the remote password. auth specifies the authorization scheme in use: e.g., password (the default), kerberos, kerberos_v5, ntlm, ssh, or any (try various in turn).

smtphost *host(s)*
> Send incoming mail to the specified host (or the first available host when the argument is a list).

preconnect *command*
postconnect *command*
> Run the specified command before/after connecting.

plugin *command*
> Use this command to make the server connection.

skip *host*
> Poll this host only when it is explicitly listed on the command line.

interval *n*
> Poll this site only on every *n*th poll (i.e., less frequently than normal).

Security

System Hardening Checklist

The following checklist summarizes the major activities that are required in order to "harden" a Unix system.

Preliminary planning

- Understand the functions that the system will be used to perform. Determine the software that will be needed.
- Plan the partition/filesystem layout with security in mind.

- Plan the system's user account and group structure.
- Gather all required software:
  - — Operating system installation media
  - — Patches to the operating system since media release
  - — Additional software packages (including any patches)
- Document the hardening process as you go.

Physical system security

- Select a location that minimizes risk from accidental damage (e.g., no overhead sprinklers).
- If appropriate, secure the physical system location with locks and other security devices.
- Secure the cabling to network and other devices.
- Install an uninterruptible power supply (UPS).
- Assign a BIOS/RAM/EEPROM password (this prevents unauthorized users from modifying settings).
- Attach any equipment identification tags/stickers to the computer and components (if applicable).

Operating system installation

- Set up disk partitioning (or logical volumes), taking into account any security considerations.
- After the initial operating system installation, apply any operating system patches that have been released since the installation media was created.
- When available, enable the high security/trusted operating system version.
- Build a custom kernel that supports only the features you need, and remove support for ones you don't need (e.g., remove IP forwarding capabilities for systems that are not operating as routers).
- Configure automatic booting so that administrator intervention is not allowed (if appropriate).
- Secure the boot loader (e.g., lilo or GRUB) with a password.
- Enable the single-user mode password if this is not the default (e.g., Red Hat Linux).

Securing local filesystems

- Look for inappropriate file and directory permissions, correcting any problems that are found. These are the most important:

  — Group- or world-writable system executables/directories

  — Group- or world-writable user home directories

  — SetUID and SetGID commands

- Select mount options for local filesystems that take advantage of any available security features (e.g., *nosuid*).

- On some systems, under some conditions, a separate */usr* filesystem can be mounted as read-only.

- Encrypt sensitive data that is present on the system.

Configuring and disabling services

- Remove or disable any unnecessary services, checking all service startup locations: */etc/inittab*, system boot scripts, and the */etc/inetd.conf* configuration file. When possible, the software for an unnecessary service should be removed.

- Use secure versions of daemons when they are available.

- If at all possible, run server processes that a special user created for that purpose and not as *root*.

- When appropriate, run servers in an isolated directory tree via the chroot facility.

- Specify a maximum number of instances for applicable servers.

- Specify access control and logging for all services:

  — Install TCP Wrappers if necessary.

  — Allow only the minimum access necessary.

  — Include an entry in */etc/hosts.deny* that denies access to everyone (so that only access explicitly granted in */etc/hosts.allow* will be permitted).

- Use any per-service user-level access control that is provided. For example, the cron and at subsystems allow you to restrict which users can use them at all. Some people recommend limiting at and cron to administrators.

- Secure all services, whether they seem security-related or not (e.g., printing).

Securing the root account

- Select a secure *root* password, and plan a schedule for changing it regularly.
- If possible, restrict the su command to a single group.
- Use sudo or system roles to grant other ordinary users limited *root* privileges when needed.
- Prevent direct *root* logins, except on the system console.

User authentication and user account attributes

- Set up the shadow password file (if necessary).
- Configure PAM as appropriate for the relevant commands.
- Define user-account password selection and aging settings.
- Set up other default user-account restrictions as appropriate (e.g., resource limits).
- Plan the system's group structure if necessary, as well as similar items such as projects.
- Set up secure default user initialization files (e.g., */etc/skel*), and the various shells' system-wide initialization files.
- Ensure that administrative and other non-login accounts have a disabled password and */bin/false* as the login shell.
- Remove unnecessary predefined accounts.

Securing remote authentication

- Disable */etc/hosts.equiv* and *.rhosts* authentication.
- Use ssh and its related commands for all remote user access. Disable rlogin, rsh, telnet, ftp, rcp, and so on.
- Configure PAM as appropriate for the relevant commands. Be sure that direct *root* access is not allowed.

Setup ongoing system monitoring

- Configure the syslog facility. Send/copy syslog messages to a central syslog server for redundancy.
- Enable process accounting.

- Install Tripwire, configure it, and record system baseline data. Write the data to removable media, and then remove it from the system. Finally, configure Tripwire to run daily.
- Design/implement a scheme for identifying important logged events. swatch is very useful for this (see page 28).

Backups

- Perform a full system backup and verify the backup media.
- Create two copies of the media.
- Plan and implement a system backup schedule.

Miscellaneous activities

- Remove any remaining source code for the kernel or additional software packages from the system.
- Add the new host to the security configuration on other systems, in router access control lists, and so on.
- Sign up for security mailing lists, if you haven't already.
- Check vendor security web page(s) on a regular basis.

Security Monitoring Commands

last   last [*users*] [*ttys*] [reboot]

Display the last login time for the specified users and/or TTYs (OR logic). reboot requests the last reboot time.

lastcomm

lastcomm [*commands*] [*users*]

Display previously run commands. Any arguments limit the display to matching items (all must be matched).

acctcom

acctcom [*options*]*AIX, HP-UX, Solaris.*

Display previously run commands. If options are used to limit the display, all items must be satisfied.

Options

-u *user*
> Limit to the specified user.

-t *tty*
> Limit to the specified TTY.

-n *pattern*
> Limit to lines containing the specified pattern.

Kernel Configuration

Default kernel location

AIX:	*/unix* (a link to */usr/lib/boot*)		
FreeBSD:	*/kernel*	HP-UX:	*/stand/vmunix*
Linux:	*/boot/vmlinuz*	Solaris:	*/kernel/genunix*

Kernel build directory

FreeBSD:	*/usr/src/sys/arch/conf*
HP-UX:	*/stand/build*
Linux:	*/usr/src/linux*

Building a custom kernel

We assume here that the kernel sources are installed and that any required patches have been applied.

FreeBSD:
```
cd /usr/src/sys/arch/conf
cp GENERIC NAME
chmod +w NAME
Edit NAME
config NAME
cd ../../compile/NAME
make depend
make
mv /kernel /kernel.save
make install
```

HP-UX: Use SAM.

| Linux: | ```
cd /usr/src/linux
cp arch/arch/config.in{,.save}
cp .config .config.save
make mrproper
make xconfig
make dep
make clean
``` |

```
edit Makefile, modify EXTRAVERSION setting
make bzImage
make install
make modules
make modules_install
```

View kernel parameters

AIX:	`lsattr -E -H -l sys0`
FreeBSD:	`sysctl -a`
HP-UX:	`sysdef`
Linux:	`cat /proc/sys/kernel/*`

Modify kernel parameters

AIX:	`chdev -l sys0 -a attribute=value`
FreeBSD:	`sysctl param=new-value`
HP-UX:	Use SAM

Configuring Boot Loaders

FreeBSD boot loader

`boot0cfg -B [-m 0xmask] disk`

Install the FreeBSD boot loader on the specified disk. *mask* is a bit mask that includes (1) or excludes (0) each successive partition.

`disklabel -B partition`

Install the boot program into the specified partition within the FreeBSD slice.
```

lilo (Linux)

```
lilo [-C config-file] [-r alternate-root] [-b partition]
```

By default, lilo installs */etc/lilo.conf* into the partition table on the system disk, using / as the root directory. Use -r when you have the desired partition mounted somewhere other than /. Use -b to specify the boot partition (this overrides the boot entry in the configuration file).

Configuration file: global settings

prompt

> Allow a user to enter a boot command.

password=*password*

> Require a password to boot (this keyword can also be used for individual boot selections).

timeout=*n*

> Wait *n*/10 seconds; then boot the default entry.

install=/boot/boot.b

> Path to second stageboot loader.

boot=*device*

> Where to install lilo (no partition=>MBR).

default=*name*

> Default image label.

message=/boot/*filename*

> Text file that is displayed before the boot prompt (recommended location).

menu-title=*string*

> Menu title.

menu-scheme=*color-specification*

> Menu color scheme.

Boot selection settings

image=*kernel-path*
> Path to kernel.

label=*name*

> Boot prompt response used to boot the specified entry.

`root=partition`
>Partition that holds the root directory (if different from the boot partition).

`table=disk`
>Use the specified partition table.

`read-only`
>Initial mount of / is read-only.

`append="string"`
>Parameters to pass to kernel.

`alias=name`
>Another label for this entry.

`other=device`
>Used instead of an image for non-Linux operating systems.

`map-drive=0x80`
>   `to=0x81`
`map-drive=0x81`
>   `to=0x80`
>Logically swap the first two disk drives (this is useful for booting Windows from the second disk).

Grand Unified Boot Loader (grub)

`grub-install [-root-directory mount-pt] '(hdn)'`

Install grub into the MBR on the specified disk. The option specifies the location of kernel images when they are stored in a separate partition from / (e.g., /boot).

Configuration file: grub.conf

Disk partition syntax

(hd*n*,*m*) is partition *m* on disk *n* (numbering starts at 0).

General settings

`splashimage (hdn,m)/grub/name.xpm.gz`
>Splash image file.

`default n`
>Default boot entry (numbering starts at 0).

timeout *secs*
> Menu timeout period.

password -md5 *encoded-password*
> Use the grub-md5-crypt command to encode the password.

Boot selection settings

title *label*
> Boot menu label.

root (hd*n*,*m*)
> Base partition (where the kernel is stored).

kernel */path* ro [root=/dev/*device*] [initrd */initrd.img*]
> Specify a Linux operating system (use root if / is on a different partition than the kernel).

makeactive
chainloader +1
> Activate the root partition, and hand the boot process off to its boot loader (used for Windows).

map (hd0) (hd1)
map (hd1) (hd0)
> Swap the first and second drives (this is useful for booting Windows from the second disk).

root (hd*n*,*m*,*x*)
kernel /boot/loader
> Boot FreeBSD partition *x* (within the FreeBSD slice).

default saved
> Remember the most recent boot selection, and make it the new default. Place the savedefault directive at the end of the stanza for each operating system for which you want to use this feature.

Index

We'd like to hear your suggestions for improving our indexes. Send email to
index@oreilly.com.